NEW JERSEY

THEN & NOW

Thunder Bay Press
An imprint of the Baker & Taylor Publishing Group
10350 Barnes Canyon Road, San Diego, CA 92121
www.thunderbaybooks.com

Produced by Salamander Books,
an imprint of Anova Books Ltd.
10 Southcombe Street, London W14 0RA, UK

"Then and Now" is a registered trademark of Anova Books Ltd.

© 2013 Salamander Books

All notations of errors or omissions should be addressed to Thunder Bay Press,
Editorial Department, at the above address. All other correspondence (author
inquiries, permissions) concerning the content of this book should be addressed
to Salamander Books, 10 Southcombe Street, London W14 0RA, UK.

Library of Congress Cataloging-in-Publication Data

Veasey, David.
  New Jersey then and now / David Veasey.
    pages cm
  ISBN-13: 978-1-60710-753-8 (hardcover)
  ISBN-10: 1-60710-753-8 (hardcover)
  1. New Jersey--Pictorial works. 2. New Jersey--History, Local--
Pictorial works. 3. Historic buildings--New Jersey--Pictorial
works. 4. Historic sites--New Jersey--Pictorial works.
  5. Repeat photography--New Jersey. I. Title.
  F135.V43 2013
  974.9--dc23
                    2012046522

Printed in China

1 2 3 4 5 17 16 15 14 13

Dedication
This book is dedicated to the "Jersey Girls" in my life: my wife, Dottie; daughter
Robyn; daughter-in-law, Jill; and granddaughter, Sarah.

Acknowledgment
A book of this nature involving a number of cities and other locations throughout
New Jersey requires the help of lots of people. I want to thank Mary Newell and
Dr. Philip Leopold at Stevens Institute of Technology for granting me access and to
Giacomo Destefano and his staff at the Paterson Museum for guiding me through
the intricacies of historic Paterson Mills. Jason Baum, of Rutgers athletic
department, was very helpful, as was pilot Stephen Lind who flew a near perfect
aerial photography mission. I want to also thank Robert Matticola of New York
Waterway and Tommy Higgins of Fort Lee municipal government. I also want to
thank archivists and librarians who aided me, Thomas Fusciano at Rutgers
University Archives and Special Collections, Joanne Nestor at the New Jersey State
Archives, Dr. George Hawley and James Lewis at the Newark Public library, and
Matt Metcalf at the Trenton Library. I also want to thank Tom Worsdale of the U.S.
Navy at Lakehurst and Thomas Feeney of the New Jersey Turnpike Authority.

NEW JERSEY
THEN & NOW

WRITTEN AND PHOTOGRAPHED BY
DAVID VEASEY

THUNDER BAY
P·R·E·S·S

San Diego, California

NEW JERSEY

THEN & NOW INTRODUCTION

New Jersey can be summed up in one word: diversity. Diversity of people, diversity of landscape, and diversity of economic activity. From sandy shores bordering the Atlantic Ocean, to rock walls of the Palisades along the Hudson River, to tree-shaded highlands, this environmental variety is packed into the nation's forty-seventh smallest state—only Connecticut, Delaware, and Rhode Island have fewer square miles.

The state's diversity of landscape is matched by its diversity of people, with ethnic groups from every major country on the globe living here, making it the most densely populated state in the union. Originally inhabited by several tribes that made up the Delaware Indian Nation, Europeans fueled the population explosion as early as 1609 when Henry Hudson explored the area and subsequent settlements were created. Dutchmen first settled into farms in Bergen, Hudson, and Middlesex counties, adjacent to the Dutch city of New Amsterdam. At the same time, British farmers filtered in from New England to Essex, Morris, and Union counties, while Quakers sought refuge in Monmouth County, and Swedes settled in Salem County. New Jersey was well-populated with multiple nationalities by 1664.

After the British defeated the Dutch in 1664, King Charles II granted all of what would become New Jersey to his brother James, Duke of York, who in turn granted the lands to George Carteret and John, Lord Berkeley. Berkeley and Carteret both conveyed their land grants to a subset of proprietors. Berkeley's lands would become West Jersey (southern New Jersey) and Carteret's claim would be East Jersey (north and central New Jersey). This act of subdivision, especially in East Jersey, would lead to centuries of court battles over land claims, with the last issue settled as recently as 1998.

In 1703 the proprietary colonies of East Jersey and West Jersey were united as the Royal Province of New Jersey. Although the colony was unified, separate capitals were maintained in Burlington (for West Jersey) and Perth Amboy (for East Jersey). The Royal Governor's house in Perth Amboy still stands and is featured in the pages of this book.

Trenton became the state capital in 1790. The city's place in New Jersey history, and U.S. history as well, was assured on Christmas night 1776 when General George Washington and his Continental Army crossed the Delaware River in a snowstorm, marched nine miles to Trenton, and defeated the Hessian garrison in the battle of Trenton. New Jersey is rightly called the Crossroads of the American Revolution because more battles and skirmishes were fought here than any other colony. Remembrances of the Revolutionary War, including the Trenton Battle Monument, Nassau Hall on the campus of Princeton University, George Washington's Headquarters in Morristown, and the Indian King Tavern in Haddonfield, are featured in the photographs herein.

The Revolutionary War spurred on the state's industrial growth as iron mining and manufacturing substituted for imported British goods. After the war, Alexander Hamilton, then Secretary of the Treasury, created the nation's first

planned industrial city in Paterson to take advantage of the waterpower of the Passaic River Falls. Water also was instrumental in the state's first major transportation system, the Morris Canal, bringing coal and iron ore to cities further facilitating industrial growth. Paterson, on the Morris Canal, was home to hundreds of mills, and also home to Rogers Locomotive Works, an important steam engine manufacturer.

The state's location between New York and Philadelphia—Benjamin Franklin's proverbial barrel tapped at both ends—was a strong spur to the economy as products manufactured here had two major cities nearby as markets. Due to its location, New Jersey became a major passenger and freight railroad center in the nineteenth and twentieth centuries. Train stations in Newark and Elizabeth are living reminders of the golden age of railway travel. Today the New Jersey Turnpike plays the primary role of linking New York to Philadelphia.

New Jersey's developed environment ranges from neo-classical buildings by noted architect Cass Gilbert in Newark, to traditional stone grist mills throughout the state. The Goldman Sachs tower on Jersey City's waterfront, aluminum-clad art deco diners, and the Gothic spires of Princeton

University are all remembered in *New Jersey Then and Now*. More than 1600 sites in the state are listed on the National Register of Historic Places, with fifty-five of those locations deemed "nationally significant in American history and culture," to merit the higher National Historic Landmark designation.

Over the years, the state has become home to pharmaceutical and computer service companies while maintaining a range of both heavy and light industry. Fishing and tourism have lasted into the twenty-first century from their eighteenth-century roots. All this diversity of economic activity frequently renders New Jersey as the nation's wealthiest state.

Change is one of life's constants. The following images focus on how New Jersey looked from 50 to 125 years in the past, and contrast the current, nearly identical views today. The sixty-eight vignettes in this book illustrate what makes New Jersey such an interesting study—the ability to adapt, and the value of preserving tradition.

Morris Canal, c. 1900

Delaware Water Gap, c. 1900

Paterson Vistas, c. 1905

Palisades Amusement Park, 1953

The Meadowlands, c. 1960

Broad Street Station, Newark, 1907

Broad Street, Newark, c. 1920

The Real Sopranos, 1935

Newark Airport, 1936

Passenger Train Service, c. 1900   p. 66

Jersey City Waterfront, 1941   p. 74

Roosevelt Stadium, c. 1940   p. 82

New Jersey Turnpike, 1953   p. 86

State House, Trenton, c. 1970   p. 96

Asbury Park, 1903   p. 114

The Hindenburg, *Lakehurst, 1935*   p. 122

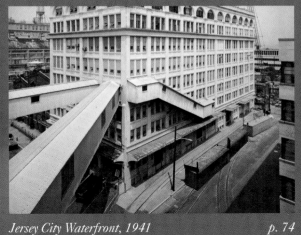

Atlantic City Boardwalk, 1938   p. 130

Lucy the Elephant, Margate, c. 1970   p. 136

1910

SUSSEX FAMILY FARM
A Dutch-styled house, home of the Foster-Armstrong family

ABOVE: The Armstrong family gathered for a wedding anniversary portrait in 1910 at the Foster-Armstrong farmhouse at 320 River Road (Old Mine Road) in Montague Township. The house was built in 1790 and the farm operated continually from then until the 1970s. Julius Foster built it in a style that is considered Dutch coastal architecture—not usually found in the Delaware Valley, although there was strong Dutch influence there. Foster's son-in-law James Armstrong added to the house in the 1820s, and by 1836 the Armstrong name became the only one associated with the house. The home is sited on one of the most famous roads in the Northeast—Old Mine Road (locally known as River Road), which ran from the Delaware Water Gap to Kingston, New York, parallel to the Delaware River for most of its 104-mile length. The date of the road's completion is subject to debate; the standard view is that it was built in 1659 by Dutch settlers to bring copper ore from the Pahaquarry Mines (Delaware Water Gap) to Kingston, New York.

ABOVE AND RIGHT: Sometime between 1910 and 1930, the second-floor balcony was removed giving the house the appearance it has today. The Foster-Armstrong house was seized under eminent domain as part of the Tocks Island Dam project that was never built, and their land subsequently became part of the Delaware Water Gap National Recreation Area. Scores of farms were seized along the river. The house was placed on the National Register of Historic Places in 1979; the Montague Association for Restoration of Community History controls it under a lease from the National Park Service. It has a small museum with local household items that were donated by area residents. One room contains Native American artifacts from the Lenni Lenape who lived nearby. Today, in light of new archaeological evidence, some historians argue that the Dutch road story is a myth and the route was an old Native American trail that linked settlements along the Delaware River, and that it wasn't made a road until the mid-1800s.

c.1900

FRANKLIN ZINC MINE

A major controlling factor in the economic development of northern New Jersey

ABOVE: The zinc mines along with related processing and smelting facilities in the Franklin Mining District, didn't become the dominant mining venture until the late 1890s when a number of smaller mines were consolidated into New Jersey Zinc Company. Earlier, from the 1700s until after the Civil War, iron ore mining was the most important hard-rock mining. Zinc mining didn't become important until more uses of zinc as an alloy were discovered. At the same time, iron mining was losing out to cheaper ores in the newly discovered Mesabi Range in Minnesota. Zinc was mined in deep tunnels with heavy-life elevators bringing the ore to the surface for processing, which took place within a half-mile of the mine. Ore was delivered by a series of conveyor belts to the smelting plant, which dominated the Franklin landscape. Iron ore and zinc occur here within marble bands that basically run under a ridge between Franklin and Ogdensburg, about one-half mile wide and five miles long.

ABOVE: Today, the Franklin mine is flooded almost to ground level, and processing plants lie in ruin with some industrial chimneys still standing as silent sentinels to a passing era. Mining ended in 1986 as a result of too-high maintenance costs—some mine shafts were 2,700 feet deep; large ore veins were depleted; and the price of zinc had dropped dramatically in the mid-1980s. Franklin sits on unique ore bodies containing some 330 different minerals, more than any place on earth. A number of those minerals are found nowhere else. Franklin is also considered the "Fluorescent Mineral Capital of the World" with many minerals that glow green, red, orange, and blue under ultraviolet light. The Franklin Mineral Museum controls a large mine tailings dump where, for a fee, one can search for rare minerals. It also has a replica mine tunnel to give visitors a glimpse of what underground mining was like. The small museum, with hundreds of fluorescent rocks on display, draws rock collectors from all over the world. Some have called the site "globally famous, locally unknown."

LEFT: Another aspect of the Franklin mine complex at the turn of the century. Today the tailings are avidly scavenged by rock collectors.

c.1900

THE MORRIS CANAL

Principal transport route for iron and coal ores during the nineteenth century

LEFT: The Morris Canal was an engineering marvel, moving boats through elevation changes of more than 1,670 feet by use of locks and incline planes in its 102-mile run from Phillipsburg, New Jersey on the Delaware River to its terminus in Jersey City on the Hudson River. Cables pulling flatbed barge carriers on the incline planes were powered by unique water turbines. The Morris Canal was promoted by Morristown businessman George P. MacCulloch, who organized the Morris Canal & Banking Company, which was granted a state charter in 1824. Canal building began a year later. The canal's primary freight was anthracite coal from Pennsylvania, and iron ore from western New Jersey was transported to Newark, Jersey City, and New York City. The canal also created a market for farmers' produce, and, in an era of few easily-traveled roads, provided vital transportation for both passengers and freight, reaching its heyday in 1866 when the canal carried 460,000 tons of coal and 291,000 tons of iron ore.

BELOW: This photograph shows one of the many incline planes used to pull barges, housed in barge carriers (right of center) from one level to another, thus negating the need for a whole flight of locks. Today it is a road.

c.1900

ABOVE AND BELOW: The canal began its long, slow decline because of competition from railroads. After years of losses the canal was finally taken over by the state in 1923 and closed two years later. Much of the canal was paved over for

Interstate 80; other sections of the canal provided the roadbed for the Newark subway system; still other parts became local streets, like Plane Street in Boonton that was used for cars instead of barges (see archive photo left). Some sections also have been preserved as parkland. The Morris Canal was not only a transport system but also altered the physical landscape by substantially enlarging Lake Hopatcong, creating Lake Musconetcong, and towns along the route, such as Port Murray, a port in name only today. The Canal is a National Engineering Landmark. The state's other major canal—Delaware and Raritan Canal, which was 44 miles in length from Bordentown on the Delaware River via Trenton to New Brunswick on the Raritan River—fared better than its northern counterpart with much of it preserved as a linear state park.

DELAWARE WATER GAP

The gap offers dramatic panoramas of the Kittatinny Ridge

c.1900

LEFT: The Delaware Water Gap is the dramatic S-shaped canyon that winds its way through the Appalachian Mountains. The area has been a popular holiday spot since the late 1800s with a number of first-class hotels on the Pennsylvania side of the river. The more rugged terrain of the New Jersey side lent itself to small campsites and cottages, not large-scale hotels. The Delaware river divides New Jersey from Pennsylvania, with ridges rising to 1,500 feet or more on either side. In New Jersey, it is called the Kittatinny Ridge, and in Pennsylvania, the Blue Mountain Ridge. The steep hills are covered in hardwood forest with hickories, ash, and maples predominant, with some pines mixed in. Black bear and white-tailed deer inhabit the area, and the river runs rich with shad, trout, and bass. The Water Gap, a cut through the mountains that is called a "notch" in New England, or in the west a "pass," was formed over the course of millennia by uplift, erosion, and glaciation.

ABOVE: The Delaware Water Gap has always been favored by tourists enjoying boating and the calm beauty of the landscape.

ABOVE: At a bend in Interstate 80, just past Columbia, New Jersey, dramatic tree-clad mountains and glistening waters of the Delaware River make motorists think they must have taken a wrong turn and are now in the mountainous West, not in New Jersey. The tranquil beauty of the Delaware Water Gap National Recreation Area hides the sad story of its creation as a national park. Over the years there had been various plans for a dam at Tocks Island in the Delaware River, six miles above the Water Gap. In 1962 Congress approved the dam and three years later created the National Recreation Area as a way to protect the future reservoir's water supply. The dam was defeated but land and farms had already been seized; these lands formed the basis of today's recreation area. The Appalachian Trail runs through the park, which includes 100 miles of hiking trails with facilities for camping, picnicking, and swimming, and there are 40 miles of river for canoeing, rafting, and kayaking.

WASHINGTON'S HEADQUARTERS

A museum celebrating Washington's Revolutionary War role

ABOVE: The Jacob Ford Mansion as it looked in 1939, just six years after becoming the nation's first National Historic Park. It was preserved as General George Washington's headquarters during the winter and spring from December 1779 to June 1780 during the Revolutionary War. A year earlier, Washington also had headquarters in Morristown at Arnold Tavern on the town green. It was these two encampments, and Washington's headquarters, that led Morristown to call itself Military Capital of the American Revolution. The home's owner, Jacob Ford, a local iron smelter, had died of pneumonia while on military duty. His widow allowed Washington and his staff to occupy most of the house while the Ford family lived in two rooms on the first floor. The house was bought at an auction in 1873 by a number of local men who formed the Washington Association of New Jersey to preserve the house as a museum. The Association donated the property to the federal government in 1933. At the time, the property was second only to Mount Vernon, Washington's Virginia home, for the number of Washington artifacts and memorabilia that it contained.

RIGHT: Detail of the doorway on the southeast side of Colonel Jacob Ford Jr.'s house.

FAR RIGHT: Main hall and stairway of the Jacob Ford Mansion.

1936

1936

ABOVE: The Georgian-style mansion was completely refurbished in 1963 and the outside was repainted white. Shutters were added to first-floor windows to make the house conform to how it looked during the Revolutionary War era. It was built of wood between 1772–1774, on a slight knoll a half mile or so from the town green. While most mansions of the period were either brick or stone, it reaches mansion status by its large grand reception hall running the length of the building and its Palladian windows framing the entrance. It is a two-and-one-half-story structure with chimneys at either end. The kitchen—as was the fashion in the day for fire safety measures—was in an outside building. All rooms are furnished with period pieces or accurate reproductions. Other units of Morristown National Historic Park include the army encampment at Jockey Hollow and a hilltop gun battery known as Fort Nonsense.

c.1865

HALFWAY HOUSE THROUGH TIME
From pre–Revolutionary War tavern to private residence, with a series of alterations

ABOVE: Halfway House in East Hanover Township was still a tavern in 1870 as it had been since the Revolutionary War era. It was owned by Colonel Ellis Cook, a member of the Eastern Battalion of Morris County Militia and also a member of the county's Committee of Safety, during the Revolutionary War. The tavern got its name from Sussex County farmers who stopped here en route to Newark markets, as the tavern was halfway between their farms and Newark. Mount Pleasant Avenue, where the house is located, was a major thoroughfare in early America. The Cook Halfway House, as it is called locally, was built in 1752 of white-painted wooden clapboard. During the Revolutionary War the bridge over the Passaic River, called Cook's Bridge, which was near the house, was important enough for the local militia to guard. A footnote to the town's history is that in 1765 the great-grandparents of inventor Thomas Edison—John Edison and Sarah Ogden—were married at a local church.

ABOVE: Halfway House as it looked under the ownership of W. Everett Rowley and his wife.

BELOW: A further evolution: Halfway House with its three newly built rooftop dormers.

ABOVE: Halfway House became a private residence sometime in the 1880s. In 1925 it was owned by W. Everett Rowley and his wife, who had the porch removed, put up the peaked two-column entryway, and added two roof dormers. By 1940 the house had three more rooftop dormers making it look close to the way it does today. The house was eventually sold to the township and it was used by the East Hanover Historical Society for meetings. A 1940 survey called the early version of the house a typical example of nineteenth-century tavern architecture. A recent booklet, *Revolutionary War Sites in Morris County*, lists Halfway House as one of eighteen important sites, along with the Ford Mansion, Jockey Hollow Soldiers' Huts, and Fort Nonsense. Halfway House at 174 Mount Pleasant Avenue in East Hanover is also the site of the Marion Rowley Gardens. The house is occasionally open to the public.

VAN DOREN MILL
From gristmill to office building

1936

ABOVE: A similar mill, the Moravian Mill in Hope, pictured in 1942. It was built 1769–1770 as a flour mill.

LEFT: The Van Doren Mill, a gristmill in Bernardsville, was still working in 1936 as it had been for more than a century. The present mill was built in 1843 by Ferdinand Van Doren, replacing a wooden mill that was built in 1768. The earlier mill had a seven-foot drop, or fall, of water. The higher the waterfall, the greater a mill's power. Van Doren wanted his new mill to be more powerful so he planned a twenty-foot waterfall. The traditional story about the mill's construction is that Van Doren hired a wandering vagrant to dig the foundation in exchange for room, board, and tobacco. The master mason who erected the mill, in about a year, was paid seventy-five cents a day; other workers on the mill's construction were paid fifty cents a day—all told, the mill cost $5,000 to build. The mill had a number of innovations including a water wheel inside the mill building. The Van Doren Mill was sold in 1929 to William Childs of the Childs restaurant family.

BELOW: Before it closed in the late 1940s, the mill was owned by William Childs. Childs, along with his brother, owned the Childs restaurant chain of more than 107 restaurants. The chain originated in New York City in 1889. Childs moved the large barn that was on the mill property across Route 202 and refurbished it into the present-day Olde Mill Inn. The mill continued to grind flour for all the Inn's baking. Customers could go over to the mill and watch flour being processed while they waited to be seated at the restaurant across the street. The mill closed in the mid-1940s and was sold in 1952 to Carl Ferenbach by the Childs estate. After being idle for more than thirty-five years the mill was sold again in 1980 to the architectural firm that designed the AT&T headquarters in Basking Ridge. They restored the mill and used it as offices while they supervised construction of the building. The mill is now owned by Innovative Educational Programs–Learning Alliances and is still used as an office building.

1935

HUNTERDON COUNTY COURTHOUSE

Scene of one of the most highly publicized trials in America

ABOVE: The famous Lindbergh kidnapping trial at the Hunterdon County Courthouse in Flemington began on January 1, 1935. As a sign of how important the state considered the trial, it was presided over by a justice of the New Jersey Supreme Court and prosecuted by the state attorney general. The trial was the result of the March 1, 1932, kidnapping of transatlantic aviator Charles A. Lindbergh's son. The kidnapper took the twenty-month-old toddler from his crib in a second-floor nursery at the family home, leaving muddy footprints on the rug. A ransom note for $50,000 was left on the windowsill. Police found a broken ladder nearby. Two months later, the child's body was discovered a short distance away from the home. After a two-year investigation led by New Jersey State Police, under its commander Colonel Norman Schwarzkopf (father of First Gulf War commander General Norman Schwarzkopf), a Bronx, New York, carpenter, Bruno Richard Hauptmann, was arrested for the crime on September 19, 1934.

1932

HAUPTMANN

A prison shot of Bruno Richard Hauptmann shortly after his conviction for the kidnapping and murder of the Lindbergh baby. The *New York Times* reported Hauptmann's conviction: "He was sentenced to die in the electric chair at the state prison in Trenton sometime during the week of March 18. The jury of eight men and four women returned its verdict after having been out for eleven hours and twenty-four minutes since it retired at 11:21 o'clock this morning (Feb 13) to deliberate in the jury room. Handcuffed to two guards, Hauptmann stood between them silent and motionless, his face ashen white and terror in his deep-set eyes, while he heard the jury state its verdict and the judge pronounced sentence."

ABOVE: The courthouse, now only used for special occasions, was silent witness to the verdict in the Lindbergh kidnapping trial, which ended on February 13, 1935, when Hauptmann was found guilty of the kidnapping and murder. He was sentenced to death the same day. He was executed on Friday, April 3, 1935, following a brief appeal. In the aftermath of the Lindbergh baby's abduction, kidnapping was made a federal crime. Lindbergh and his wife moved to Europe for several years after the trial to get away from the intense publicity the trial generated. The Lindberghs returned to the United States in April 1939. Lindbergh was against United States participation in World War II, but after the attack on Pearl Harbor he served as an air power consultant. The courthouse was used regularly until 1996 when a new justice complex was built for the Hunterdon County Court.

FAR LEFT AND LEFT: Scene of the crime: the Lindbergh home, on an 800-acre estate in Hopewell, was completed in 1932. The house was isolated with a driveway of three-quarters of a mile leading from a country lane to the house.

1900

PASSAIC FALLS
The second-highest waterfall east of the Mississippi River

ABOVE: An aerial view of the hydroelectric plant. The early raceway system drew water from the Passaic River through a dam above the falls.

LEFT: Passaic River Falls at Paterson has attracted visitors ever since two Dutch travelers wrote about them in 1679. Alexander Hamilton, first U.S. Secretary of the Treasury, considered them as a source of waterpower. He later created the Society for Useful Manufactures (SUM), America's first planned industrial complex to harness the falls. The society was granted New Jersey business license number one on November 22, 1791. By 1836 the SUM had built a system of sluices and raceways to bring water for power to many mills producing everything from guns to textiles to beer. The Great Falls, as it is also called, is second to Niagara Falls as the highest waterfall east of the Mississippi River. The Passaic River plunges seventy-seven feet in Paterson as it slices through the Watchung Mountains.

ABOVE: The Great Falls and related sites were declared a National Historic Landmark in 1976, designated a National Civil Engineering Landmark in 1977, a state park in 2004, and on November 7, 2011 the site was officially made America's 397th national park. The intricate system of waterways that powered mills is still largely intact. The first system of raceways was designed by Pierre Charles L'Enfant, the French architect who designed Washington, D.C. One of the best preserved buildings in the national park is the Erecting Shop, home of the Paterson Museum, once part of a dozen buildings of Rogers Locomotive Works. The Works were powered by water from the upper raceway. While the Great Falls no longer provides energy for mills, they have generated hydroelectric power since 1912.

PATERSON VISTAS

Panoramic views of the Passaic River and the heart of "Silk City"

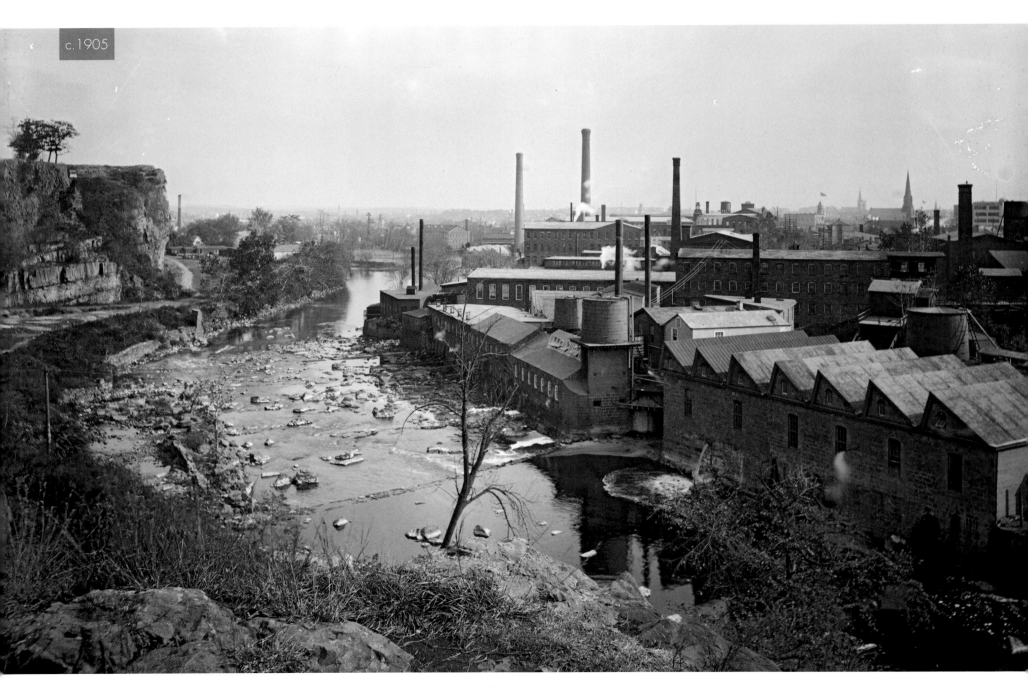

c.1905

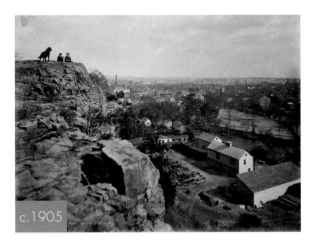

c.1905

The concentration of factories and workers led to a number of clashes between labor and mill owners. The most famous was a 1913 strike demanding an eight-hour workday, improved working conditions, and protection against technological change that threatened jobs. The strike garnered national attention, with the Industrial Workers of the World union—called the wobblies—involved in the strike. Police arrested more than 1,800 strikers. The police response sparked demonstrations and national fund-raising efforts on behalf of the strikers with vigils held in a number of cities. Pietro and Maria Botto House in the neighboring town of Haledon served as strike headquarters, and today is a National Historic Landmark and has a small American Labor Museum. Workers were considered to have lost the strike. They gained the eight-hour workday in 1919.

LEFT: Paterson was a thriving industrial center in 1905 with mills strung along the Passaic River, although coal, not water, powered many of them. Paterson can trace its roots as the first planned industrial town in America from Alexander Hamilton's Society of Useful Manufactures, an attempt to create a manufacturing base in the United States to compete with England's industrial prowess. Paterson had in excess of a hundred textile mills processing cotton and other fibers, as well as the Colt Gun Mill and Rogers Locomotive Works. The city began to specialize in textiles in the mid-1800s, especially silk. By the late nineteenth century, Paterson was known as "the Silk City," which had become the dominant fiber because of the city's close proximity to the major market of New York City. The pure, soft water of the Passaic River was ideal for silk dyeing, and there was a plentiful supply of cheap labor. By 1900 the silk industry employed 30,000 workers in New Jersey, two-thirds of them in the 175 mills and dyeing companies of Paterson.

BELOW: The decline of the mills came about for several interrelated reasons—competition from cheaper wage areas in the United States, outdated factories, and use of artificial fabrics such as rayon.

ABOVE: A view from farther along the bluff looking out across America's first planned industrial city.

ABOVE RIGHT: The city has attempted to revitalize the area in recent years, including the installation of period lamp posts and the conversion of old industrial buildings into apartments.

c.1925

WARD AND MAIN STREETS, PATERSON

The city was created in 1792 by the governor of New Jersey, William Paterson

LEFT: The intersection at Ward and Main streets was busy in 1925, as Paterson's downtown business and retail shopping district thrived. The Morrissee Building, with a billboard on its roof, is a good example of the Renaissance Revival style. It was designed by Paterson architect Charles Edwards and built in 1892 of buff-colored brick. The original owner James A. Morrissee, a well-known real estate broker and developer, had his headquarters in the building. The building passed out of family ownership in 1917 to a paint company, followed by a variety of other businesses. The Morrissee Building anchored a major downtown corner of the city founded by Alexander Hamilton. The city is named after William Paterson, delegate to the Constitutional Convention, governor of New Jersey from 1790–1793, and creator of his namesake city in 1792 when he signed a charter bringing it into existence.

ABOVE: The downtown corner of Ward and Main streets, with ground-level stores in a five-story office building that still anchors the busy corner. The Morrissee Building, the previous anchor building, was taken over by the Paterson Redevelopment Agency in 1970. At that time its condition was described as fair. It was demolished in 1987 to make way for the new office building and stores. Like all aging urban centers in New Jersey and throughout the Northeast, shopping malls with their acres of free parking have decimated downtown businesses as shoppers drive to their destinations instead of taking trains or parking downtown. Major department stores also left the cities, spurring further decay, as they were replaced with dollar and other discount stores. Downtown Paterson was placed on the National Register of Historic Places in 1999.

1932

GEORGE WASHINGTON BRIDGE
The longest suspension bridge in the world at the time of its construction in 1931

TOP: Ceremonial parade for the opening of the Hudson River Bridge in October 1931. It was later renamed the George Washington Bridge.

ABOVE: The floodlit George Washington Bridge stands majestically over the Hudson river.

LEFT: Soon after its opening in 1931, leading modernist architect Le Corbusier described the George Washington Bridge as "the most beautiful bridge in the world. Made of cables and steel beams, it gleams in the sky like a reversed arch. It is blessed." The bridge's chief engineer was Othmar Amman, who is often called the bridge's designer. However, noted architect Cass Gilbert was involved with the bridge's design, although that is rarely mentioned. The bridge is 3,500 feet across from tower to tower, suspended 250 feet above the Hudson River, connecting Fort Lee, New Jersey with the Washington Heights neighborhood in Manhattan. When it was built, it was the longest suspension bridge in the world. It cost $60 million and used 107,000 miles of steel wire strands spun into four high tensile strength cables, each a yard in diameter. The wire cable was furnished by Trenton's premier steel-cable manufacturer Roebling & Sons Co.

ABOVE: The bridge has fourteen lanes for traffic; the first expansion was in 1946 when the center median was paved over adding two more lanes to the original six-lane bridge. A lower deck designed by Othmar Amman was added in 1962, containing six more lanes. Satirists have called this addition the Martha Washington Bridge. The "GWB"—as it is known locally—is a vital transportation link between New England and the states south and west of New York City, by way of the New Jersey Turnpike and Interstate 95. In 2010, 51.2 million vehicles paid to cross the bridge going eastbound (so the total number of cars using the bridge is likely double that amount), while in its first full year of operation at the end of 1932, 5.5 million vehicles used the bridge. The current cash toll is $12, collected only on eastbound traffic, and is a far cry from the initial toll of fifty cents. Toll pass holders are offered a discount. It is little known that the bridge has sidewalks for bicycles and pedestrians; use of the sidewalks is free of charge.

1953

PALISADES AMUSEMENT PARK

A popular amusement park from the 1930s through the 1960s, now the site of apartments

ABOVE: Palisades Amusement Park, in 1947, covered thirty-eight acres on the Palisades rock formation in the towns of Fort Lee and Cliffside Park. The park began life in 1898 as a picnic spot and small amusement park operated by the local trolley company to increase weekend business. Over the years, a subsequent owner added a 1.5-million-gallon saltwater pool and other attractions. In 1935, at the height of the Great Depression, the Rosenthal brothers bought the fledging enterprise and turned it into a successful amusement park.

There is no accurate count of all the various rides over the years with rides regularly added and dropped, although the famous Cyclone roller coaster and the saltwater pool were always favorites. A serious fire in 1944 killed seven and injured 150 people. The park was given priority in getting scarce wartime material to rebuild because it was considered an essential entertainment for servicemen. The park was well known for sponsoring concerts starting with Benny Goodman in the 1930s and continuing into the 1960s.

1950

RIGHT: Today the Winston Towers apartments in Fort Lee stands in the middle of three apartment complexes that replaced Palisades Amusement Park after it closed on September 12, 1971. The park was a victim of its own success as crowds flocked there, especially to its concerts in the 1950s and 1960s, hosted by popular disk jockeys. Neighboring towns couldn't handle the volume of traffic so Fort Lee and Cliffside Park rezoned the park for apartments. Irving, the sole surviving Rosenthal brother, in poor health, sold the park. A small plaque by a bus stop at Winston Towers quotes popular Top-40 disk jockey, Cousin Brucie (Bruce Morrow), who hosted concerts at the park, "Here we were happy, here we grew! This is dedicated to the men and women who worked and played at Palisades Amusement Park, especially to the man who was its spirit, its shaker and mover, Irving Rosenthal." The small plaque (above) and a PBS documentary *Palisades Amusement Park: a Century of Fond Memories*, are all that remain of the park.

LEFT: Aerial view of Palisades Amusement Park showing the roller coaster and saltwater swimming pool.

c.1960

THE MEADOWLANDS
An unregulated dumpsite was transformed into a football stadium

LEFT: The vast area known as the Meadowlands in Bergen, Passaic, and Hudson counties is the remnant of glacial Lake Hackensack, a product of the Ice Age 20,000 years ago, when glaciers retreated leaving a lake that gradually filled in with rich soil and plants, creating today's meadowlands. In the 1700s and 1800s, cedar logging and hay farming took over much of the marsh. Brickmaking was an important industry based on rich beds of clay. The meadowlands also became an unregulated dumpsite forcing the state to finally take action to stop it. The 1969 Hackensack Meadowlands Reclamation and Development Act was designed to stop dumping as well as promote development. Among other things, the law created Hackensack Meadowlands Commission. A New Jersey forest firefighter told of battling a fire in the Meadowlands where the flames were blue and orange—something never seen in a forest fire where smoke is white or black—a sure sign that the fire was fueled by chemicals mixed with the flaming brush.

ABOVE: The stadium is the second one on the site in East Rutherford. It is now called MetLife Stadium replacing Giants Stadium that was torn down in 2009. The stadium was built by New Jersey Sports & Exhibition Authority, which was created in 1971 to develop the Meadowlands into a sports and entertainment complex. The goal was to provide a racetrack and a stadium home for the New York Giants football team. The first stadium opened in October 1976. The racetrack (bottom left), which features thoroughbred and harness racing, opened in September 1977. An indoor arena was added in 1981, which was home to the New Jersey Devils hockey team until their move to the Prudential Center arena in Newark. The arena also housed the Nets basketball team before they moved to Newark, and then to Brooklyn. The East Rutherford sports complex has its own exit on the New Jersey Turnpike and its own New Jersey Transit rail station. A large-scale shopping mall has been under construction intermittently for a number of years.

1936

PRESIDENT GROVER CLEVELAND
Birthplace of the twenty-second and twenty-fourth president of the United States

ABOVE: Jersey boy Grover Cleveland was born in this house in Caldwell on March 18, 1837, and lived here until he was four years old. His parents then moved to upstate New York. Cleveland, a New York attorney, came into the national spotlight after he was elected mayor of Buffalo in 1882. He was an energetic reformer going after corrupt political machines and insisting on honest government. His reform efforts attracted statewide attention that led to his election as governor in 1883. His anticorruption reputation was such that he was nominated Democratic Party candidate for president in 1884. Cleveland won but lost his reelection bid in 1888—although he won the popular vote, Benjamin Harrison had more electoral college votes. Cleveland won the 1892 election against Harrison, thus becoming the only U.S. president to serve nonconsecutive terms. His birthplace was bought by a group of Cleveland's supporters and opened to the public in 1913. It became a state park in 1930.

1930

TOP: The house as it could be seen in 1930, when it became a state park. It was enlarged several times between 1848–1870 to meet the growing needs of the Presbyterian clergy. The house is a good example of local vernacular architecture.

ABOVE AND LEFT: The house at 207 Bloomfield Avenue was repainted buff color for an unknown reason about a decade ago. It was painted white for years, which is believed to be the original color. The first floor of the two-story main house, with a one-story kitchen wing, serves as a museum displaying Cleveland memorabilia, and features rooms restored with period furniture. It was enlarged several times between 1848 and 1870. His original crib is located in the nursery. The house, built in 1832, shows no physical sign that it was once the parsonage for the First Presbyterian Church where Cleveland's father,

Reverand Richard Farley Cleveland, was minister from 1834–1841. Cleveland's legacy is that he was considered honest, independent, and one who strengthened the powers of the presidency; he paved the way for the modern role of president, but he was one who had no real vision for the country. The Grover Cleveland Birthplace, also known as Caldwell Presbyterian Church Manse, was listed on the National Register of Historic Places in 1977.

1970

NEW JERSEY DINERS
New Jersey could be renamed the Diner State

ABOVE: The Salem Oak Diner on West Broadway in Salem was placed at its current site in 1955. It is a manufactured building, as are all traditional diners. It was built in Paterson by the Silk City Diner Company. Robert McAlister's father won $50,000 at a Philadelphia horse racetrack in September 1955, and the next day drove to Paterson and bought the diner. The family owned it from 1955 to 2006. The son took over the diner in 1966 and ran it until 2006 when he sold it to Christina Zervas. The Silk City Diner

Company was the subsidiary of Paterson Vehicle Company, which also made truck and bus bodies. The company made diners from 1927 until it went out of business in 1964. The company was the first to mass produce diners, building six to eight at a time using a variety of color schemes.

1943

LEFT: The Art Deco structure of the Valley Diner in Upper Montclair contradicts the dictionary definition of a diner as a restaurant usually resembling a (railroad) dining car in shape. A true diner is a manufactured building.

ABOVE: The Salem Oak Diner looks pretty much the same as it did in the early 1970s. While the diner was invented in Providence, Rhode Island, in 1872, New Jersey is known for its diners and could legitimately be called the Diner State. At one time in the 1990s, the state had approximately 600 diners, more than any other state. There has been no recent diner count. New Jersey diners have been prominently featured on the popular Food Network programs, "Diners, Drive-ins and Dives," and "The Best Thing I Ever Ate." Lonely Planet's guidebook, *USA's Best Trips*, under offbeat travel, also has a section on New Jersey diners. The famous Salem oak tree, for which the diner is named, is still across the street as it has been supposedly since 1675, but it looks like a geriatric case with wires and supports propping up its ancient limbs.

1963

THOMAS EDISON HOUSE
Home of the creator of the first film studio, the phonograph, and many more inventions

ABOVE: Prolific inventor and industrialist Thomas Edison was a prime mover in New Jersey industry. He transferred his "invention factory," as he called his workshops and laboratories, from Menlo Park, where he had established the world's first industrial research facility, to larger quarters in West Orange in 1887. At West Orange, in 1893, he created the Black Maria, the first film studio, and he is considered the father of the American film industry, making such classics as *The Great Train Robbery*. In a front-page article on October 18, 1931, announcing Edison's death, *The New York Times* called him a "...creative genius (who) gave the world the electric light, the phonograph, the motion picture camera, and a thousand other inventions ranging through all the various fields of science." The holder of more individual patents than any other person in history was another accolade for Edison (true until 2003). He died, age eighty-four, at his estate in the Llewellyn Park section of West Orange.

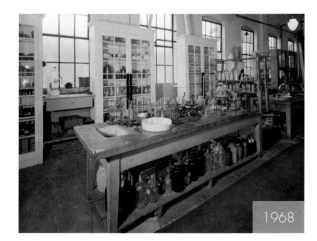

1968

RIGHT: Apparatus displayed approximately as it was during the late 1920s, when Edison conducted a series of experiments on rubber extraction from the goldenrod plant.

EDISON'S GLENMONT ESTATE

Thomas Edison, reading a newspaper in 1917, at his Glenmont Estate, the twenty-nine-room mansion in the gated community of Llewellyn Park. It was designed by architect Henry Hudson Holly, who also designed Edison's nearby laboratory complex. The mostly wooden structure, painted brick red, is done in Queen Anne style, a speciality of the architect. The ornate interior featured elegant ceilings that were hand-painted, sumptuous chandeliers, and a variety of stained glass windows. The mansion was originally built for Henry C. Pedder, an executive with Arnold Constable Department Store. It remained empty after it became known that Pedder built the house with money he had embezzled from his employer. The Edisons bought the house in 1886. Edison's second wife, Mina Miller, ran the estate calling herself the "home executive." He sold the mansion to her in 1891 to avoid possible confiscation by creditors following reverses in his iron mining operations in Ogdensburg, New Jersey.

RIGHT: The Edison National Historic Park in West Orange reopened in September 2009 after being closed for seven years for major renovations and expansion of exhibits. The $13 million makeover opened Edison's original music recording studio and his private laboratory for the first time. Many rooms had original furnishings installed. The historic buildings also had updates with new heating and air-conditioning systems, new alarms, and structural repairs. Edison was not only an inventor but also an industrialist who manufactured many of the items he invented. His company Edison General Electric Company merged with the Thomson-Houston Electric Company to form the General Electric Company, a globally significant company to this day.

1963

ABOVE: Edison's laboratories on Main Street and Lakeside Avenue in West Orange in 1963, shortly after they were made into a National Historic Park on September 5, 1962.

c.1930

BRANCH BROOK PARK
America's oldest county park

ABOVE: Branch Brook Park as it looked in the late 1930s. It had expanded to 359 acres from its sixty-acre beginning as an enclave in north Newark. It was the first acquisition in the newly established Essex County Park Commission in 1895, the nation's first county park system, making Branch Brook the nation's oldest county park. The park's first designer was the landscape architectural firm of Bogart and Barrett, who planned a series of European-style formal gardens. They were replaced in 1898 by the Olmsted Brothers, started by the nephew and stepson of Frederick Law Olmsted, the nation's leading landscape architect, who added many of the features one sees today. While the park looks like preserved woods, meadows, streams, and lakes, it was actually a highly artificial creation with man-made lakes, earthen mounds to create higher ground, and planting of hundreds of trees, shrubs, and flowers, using elements from nature to create the natural-looking park. The Olmsted style featured winding roads, streams, lakes, open fields, and scenic overlooks.

ABOVE: The park is known today for its cherry blooms, whose trees were a gift of the Bamberger department store family to the park in 1927. The park has more than 2,000 cherry trees, making it the largest display of cherry blossoms in the country—even more than the famous Washington, D.C., spring display. The park today encompasses 359 acres, adjacent to Sacred Heart Cathedral, and is named after a brook that flowed through it into the Passaic River. The park was placed on the National Register of Historic Places in 1981. It recently underwent a $25 million rehabilitation of bridges, roadways, baseball fields, and park buildings. More cherry trees were also planted. The park has similarities to Prospect Park in Brooklyn, New York, also designed by Olmsted, with a main lake, winding roads, and open meadows.

c.1935

SACRED HEART CATHEDRAL

The only French-style Cathedral in the United States

LEFT: Sacred Heart Cathedral is the seat of the archdiocese of Newark and the state's only large-scale European-style Catholic Cathedral, shown here in the mid-1930s before it was completed. The cornerstone had been laid in 1899. The Cathedral's first designer was architect Jeremiah O'Rourke who conceived a Gothic cathedral that would soar ten stories high and be 365 feet long with a nave width of 50 feet—the same dimensions of today's cathedral. Conflict between the architect and contractor over safety of certain design elements and countercharges of contract violations led to a halt in construction in 1908 and O'Rourke's removal as architect in 1910. Later that same year, Isaac E. Ditmars was named architect. He changed the design to French Gothic in a style that is reminiscent of Chartres Cathedral in France, although here both 232-foot front towers are symmetrical. Construction resumed in 1913.

c.1930

ABOVE: The cathedral was not considered finished until 1950, and would not formally be dedicated until October 19, 1954. It is built of Vermont granite, with a large stained glass window in the center of the basilica between its two towers. Interior design elements include a series of chapels with beautifully rendered stained glass windows. The central aisle of the nave is 148 feet long and 100 feet high, lined with pillars supporting graceful vaults. It is a dramatic

LEFT: A work in progress until 1950, the cathedral veered between two ornate Gothic styles but ended up as French Gothic.

space that never fails to impress visitors. Pope John Paul II celebrated evening prayers at the Cathedral in 1995 during his U.S. visit. The cathedral's formal name is Cathedral Basilica of the Sacred Heart, and it was placed on the National Register of Historic Places in 1976. The cathedral offers services in both English and Spanish. The church was funded entirely by its parishioners, who were mostly immigrants working in the factories and other businesses of Newark. Most Roman Catholic churches in New Jersey were designed for their Irish, Italian, and Polish parishioners, so the French Gothic design is distinctive.

1907

BROAD STREET STATION, NEWARK

This DL&W station served both commuters and long-distance rail travelers

ABOVE: Newark's Broad Street Station was one of several attractive stations the Delaware Lackawanna & Western Railroad (DL&W) put up in the early 1900s to serve its growing number of commuter train passengers. Broad Street Station was designed by the railroad's architect, Frank Nies, in a Renaissance Revival style using elegant brick and stone. The attractive 80-foot clock tower on the eastbound side of the station faces Broad Street as a beacon to Newark travelers. The station was built in 1903 replacing the Morris & Essex Station one block east. Commuter rail service started in 1837 between Morristown and

Newark, but it wasn't until 1907, following construction of the DL&W Hoboken Terminal, that fast commuter trains were inaugurated, making it practical for the first time to live in New Jersey and work in New York City. The Hoboken station was a transportation hub with streetcars and ferryboats. Broad Street Station also served long-distance travelers, as it was an important stop on the railroad's service to Buffalo, New York.

ABOVE: The former DL&W railroad station was spruced up from 2004 to 2008; years of grime were removed from its facade and interior spaces, along with major infrastructure upgrades. The station is served by Newark's light railway system. Broad Street Station has changed hands a number of times. It was owned by the DL&W from 1903 to 1960. Because of declining coal revenues and mounting commuter rail costs, the DL&W merged with its arch rival—the Erie Railroad—in 1960, becoming the Erie-Lackawanna. That combined railroad went bankrupt, as did a number of Eastern railroads, which led to the creation of Conrail in 1976 as a U.S. government–sponsored corporation to own the ailing railroads. New Jersey Transit took over commuter rail operations and most of its stations in 1983. The station, with the tallest campanile-style clock tower in Newark, was placed on the National Register of Historic Places in 1984. The overhead electrical wires running through the station have been there since 1930 when the Morris & Essex branch was electrified from Hoboken to Dover.

c.1910

NEWARK STREETSCAPE
From major transportation center to popular shopping area

ABOVE: Passengers wait on the safety island at the trolley stop in front of Stoutenburgh's Clothing Store at 805 Broad Street in Newark. The trolley approaching was a Broad Street Division trolley of Public Service Corp, which had consolidated all Newark trolleys into its gas and electricity operations in 1903. By 1910 more than 550 trolleys an hour passed through the Broad and Market street intersection, the heart of downtown Newark. Stoutenburgh & Co.'s clothing store, directly behind the trolley stop, was in business from 1849

until 1917. It moved into the Broad Street building in 1875 after outgrowing its location opposite the Episcopal Cathedral where the business was started. The new building had more than 325,000 square feet within its four stories. The first floor was the main sales floor; other floors contained boys clothes, specialty departments, offices, and a manufacturing floor. The company employed 200 people in 1917. The medieval-looking high-rise in the background is the Prudential Insurance Co. headquarters put up in 1892.

48

ABOVE: The 800 block on Broad Street is still recognizable today. The Stoutenburgh & Co.'s clothing store now has a Payless shoe store and a pizzeria on the ground floor. The other floors of 805 Broad Street are used as offices. The Prudential Insurance Company building is still in the background, with the 1960 high-rise replacing the old 1898 building. In the same manner, buses replaced trolley cars downtown in the 1950s. In 1910, when the city was a bustling shopping destination with at least three major department stores, it had a population of 347,000. Today it has a population of 247,000. A combination of factors led to the city's decline, but business and residential flight was accelerated by the riots from July 12–17, 1967, that left twenty-two dead and millions of dollars in damages. Some buildings have been empty since then. Newark is slowly making a comeback with the Prudential Center and New Jersey Performing Arts Center, once again luring people from the suburbs downtown.

c.1920

BROAD STREET, NEWARK
The historic heart of downtown Newark

LEFT: Broad Street plays the role of New York City's Fifth Avenue, its Broadway, and its Eighth Avenue transportation hub. Two of the three high-rise buildings, from right to left, are still standing. The first is National State Bank Building at 810, designed by noted architect Cass Gilbert and built in 1912. It is a limestone-clad, twelve-story steel-frame building. It was listed on the National Register of Historic Places in 1977. The other building is the Kinney Building at 790 Broad Street, a twelve-story office building completed in 1913 and also designed by Cass Gilbert. Both buildings are considered to be a neoclassical style. Gilbert was considered a conservative "who believed architecture should reflect historic traditions and the established social order," as one architectural critic described him. He is known for his Beaux-Arts style. Among his famous buildings are: the Woolworth Building, the U.S. Courthouse, the Alexander Hamilton Customs House—all in lower Manhattan, as well as other buildings in Newark.

RIGHT: The building at 810 Broad Street is the historic National State Bank Building that is being converted into a 106-room hotel, the Hotel Indigo. The hotel is within walking distance to the Prudential Center for sporting and cultural events. Another hotel—only a block away, on Broad Street—opened as a Courtyard by Marriott. The hotels are a sign that downtown Newark is rebounding under the impact of the Prudential Center and New Jersey Performing Arts Center a few blocks away. The Kinney building at 790 Broad Street sits empty. It has stores on its ground floor but entry to the upper floors was blocked at the time of writing.

c.1935

CATHEDRAL AND GRIFFITH BUILDING, NEWARK

Mrs. Parker Griffith, of the Griffith Piano Company, was dubbed a "one-woman cultural center"

ABOVE: Broad Street, Newark's major artery, has always been a mixed-use area. The building on the right in the mid-1930s—the Griffith Plaza Building—was designed by architect George Elwood Jones in a Gothic style that rises more than seventeen stories. It was built in 1927 for the Griffith Piano Company and opened June 1, 1928.

The piano company at 605 Broad Street called itself the "music center of New Jersey." The company sold pianos, organs, and other musical instruments, from the late 1920s until the late 1950s. Across the street is the Episcopal Cathedral of Newark, making Newark one of the few cities with two cathedrals. (Sacred Heart is the other.)

Trinity Cathedral is Newark's second-oldest religious building, after First Presbyterian Church, also on Broad Street. The Episcopal Cathedral was chartered by the Church of England in 1746. Part of the tower dates from 1743, but most of the present church was built in 1810. It was designed by Captain Josiah James, a parishioner.

ABOVE: The high-rise buildings behind the Episcopal Cathedral are two of Newark's iconic skyscrapers, closest to the steeple is the Lefcourt Building, now an apartment building, and beyond is the National Newark & Essex Bank Building. Across the street from the cathedral is the Griffith Building, which had its own 400-seat auditorium on the second floor. It was a musical and cultural center bringing in renowned classical musicians to perform under the auspices of a foundation created by Mrs. Parker Griffith. One historian has called her a one-person New Jersey Performing Arts Center. She and the foundation played an important cultural role in the city until the business closed in the 1950s. Trinity Cathedral was designated the cathedral for the archdiocese of Newark in 1944. It is the nation's oldest cathedral building. Its formal name is Trinity & St. Philip's Cathedral Episcopal. It merged with St. Philip's church in 1966; the cathedral was listed on the National Register of Historic Places in 1972. The cathedral is still functioning, while the Griffith Building lies idle today.

FEDERAL BUILDING, NEWARK

Home of the federal courts in Newark since 1936

1936

BELOW: The area around the 1936 federal building has evolved into a government complex, now called Federal Square, although local street addresses are also used. Most court activity has gravitated to the new Martin Luther King Jr. Courthouse, behind the original building. The 1936 building still serves the functions it was designed for, that is courtrooms are still on the third and fourth floors. The official name of the federal courts in New Jersey is the United States District Court for the District of New Jersey.

The district is one of the original thirteen courts established in 1789. The main post office and other government offices are still there. The building was renamed Frank R. Lautenberg Post Office and Courthouse on October 23, 2000, after New Jersey's U.S. senator who was first elected to the Senate in 1982. At his urgings a large plaque was put in the entranceway with the inscription: "The true measure of democracy is its dispensation of justice."

LEFT AND ABOVE: The U.S. federal building housed courts, the post office, and other government offices. It was opened for business on March 30, 1936, replacing an 1896 building that was located at Newark's crossroads of Market and Broad streets. The federal courts convened there from 1913 to 1936, moving into the consolidated federal building on its opening. The five-story federal building is bounded by Franklin, Mulberry, and Walnut streets, one block from Broad Street. The first and second floors were used by the post office, the third and part of the fourth floor contained U.S. courts, and the fifth floor had the Treasury Department and other federal agencies. The building cost $6,150,000 and its chief architect was William E. Lehman, who designed it in a style called Italian Classical, a type used for U.S. Treasury Department buildings in that time period. The WPA* Guide to New Jersey called it a "ponderous neoclassical structure."

* Works Progress Administration, a depression-era government program that assisted the unemployed.

1935

THE REAL *SOPRANOS*

Gangsters and organized crime were operating in New Jersey long before the popular television series

ABOVE: The Palace Chop House, on 12 East Park Street, near Broad Street in downtown Newark, was the obscure steakhouse where notorious gangster Dutch Schultz was gunned down on October 24, 1935. He was living at the Military Park Hotel, around the corner, after moving his bootlegging and numbers games to Newark from New York City, after New York authorities began cracking down on his illegal activities. Front-page headlines in *The New York Times* the next day tell of his death: "Schultz Dies of Wounds Without Naming Slayers: 3 Aides Dead, One Dying: Shot in Abdomen Fatal." The murders were second to Chicago's St. Valentine's Day massacre for violence. At the time of his death, Schultz was under federal investigation for tax evasion and was shunned by fellow gangsters as a publicity seeker. Some observers have speculated that his weakened position sparked gang warfare that led to his death. Schultz, whose real name was Arthur Flegenheimer, was born in the Bronx and got his nickname from a local tough guy that he emulated.

RIGHT: Gang overlord Ruggiero Boiardo, in pinstripes, celebrates the treaty signed between himself and Abe Zwillman, boss racketeer of Newark's Third Ward.

1930

ABOVE: The Palace Chop House was torn down in 2008 to make way for a parking lot, its only tangible remains is a sidewalk plaque detailing events that unfolded here in 1935. Over the years, the building housed a pizzeria, a dry cleaners, and at the time of its demolition the ground floor was vacant. Former Governor Brendan Byrne at one time suggested the building should be restored to its original 1935 condition and be used as a period restaurant tourist attraction. While the *Sopranos* series caught American fancy, real-life mobsters have been part of New Jersey for generations and aren't glamorous, as anyone who knew about the famous FBI-recorded mob tapes in the late-1960s knows. The tapes were widely reported in newspapers. Mobsters were taped discussing how their sons were stealing suitcases from cars at New Jersey Turnpike rest areas, among other less-than-glamorous activities.

1935

BAMBERGER'S DEPARTMENT STORE
Part of a revolution in retail shopping

ABOVE: Bamberger's Department Store was one of the country's earliest large department stores, which, along with R. H. Macy and Marshall Fields in Chicago, changed the face of retail shopping by offering a wide variety and assortment of goods under one roof. The company was founded in 1892 by Louis Bamberger, Louis Frank, and Felix Fuld. Its eleven-story flagship store at 131 Market Street in Newark was built in 1913. The store's architect was Jarvis Hunt who also designed the Newark Museum, a gift of Bamberger's to the city. Merchandise was displayed from the basement, which served as a discount center and tearoom, to the seventh floor. Higher floors were used for company offices.

ABOVE: Bamberger's, New Jersey's premier department store for decades, is largely idle with only its ground floor occupied by various retail outlets. Bamberger's former flagship store was closed in 1991 after years of declining sales. The name Bamberger's hasn't been used since 1986 when all the company's New Jersey stores were rebranded as Macy's—Macy's bought Bamberger's in 1929 after the death of founder Felix Fuld, but continued using the Bamberger's brand. The name lives on in other ways. Radio Station WOR in New York City was founded by Bamberger's in 1922 as a platform to advertise the store's wares, with studios on the sixth floor of the retail store building. It was called Bamberger's Broadcasting Service, and in the mid-1930s Bamberger's created the Mutual Broadcasting Network, one of the four national radio networks that lasted from the 1930s to the 1980s. Bamberger's also created the popular annual Thanksgiving Day parade that is broadcast on television nationally under the Macy's banner.

c.1930

ESSEX COUNTY COURTHOUSE

Backdrop to a Lincoln statue from the same sculptor responsible for the Mount Rushmore busts

ABOVE: The elegant lines of the Essex County courthouse were designed by renowned architect Cass Gilbert in a Beaux-Arts style. Gilbert was also the architect for the U.S. Supreme Court building. The five-story, marble-clad courthouse cost $2 million. The inside space is dominated by a dramatic four-story rotunda with a Tiffany-glass skylight. The building, on Springfield and Market streets in Newark, was built in 1906 to house all Essex County government offices. In the plaza at the front of the courthouse is the famous statue of Abraham Lincoln seated on a bench, created by Gutzon Borglum in 1911. The statue was dedicated by President Teddy Roosevelt on May 31, 1911. Gutzon has another impressive sculpture in Newark—the Wars of America in Military Park—however, he is best known for creating the monumental busts of four U.S. presidents on Mount Rushmore in South Dakota. He was once asked why he placed Lincoln at the end of the bench. He replied that Lincoln was the type of man who would gladly share a bench.

ABOVE: In 2004 the $49 million renovation of the historic Essex County Courthouse was completed. On the outside, masonry was cleaned and repointed, decorative elements were repaired; inside the building statuary, murals, and other artworks were restored. Behind the scenes, all utilities, fire control systems, passenger elevators, and other building systems were modernized. The building has resumed looking like a New Jersey version of the Parthenon in Athens, from its hilltop perch overlooking the downtown business district, although the hill in Newark isn't as dramatic as the one in Athens. The courthouse was added to the National Register of Historic Places in 1975. There is a small-scale version of "Seated Lincoln" at the Newark Museum. Essex County courts have long outgrown their original building and now have two other courthouses for their sixty judges. They are the nearby Veterans Courthouse and the Robert N. Wilentz Justice Center.

PENNSYLVANIA STATION, NEWARK

A major transportation hub since the 1930s—and one of the grand Penn stations that wasn't demolished

1935

LEFT: Pennsylvania Station at Raymond Plaza and Market streets, Newark, was dedicated in 1935. It is a Beaux-Arts style station designed by the well-known architectural firm of McKim, Mead, and White, whose other notable buildings include Brooklyn Museum, the James Farley Post Office, and the original Penn Station in New York City. The station has an impressive waiting room with marble walls featuring emblems tracing the history of transportation from a Viking ship to an airplane. The station was erected while the Pennsylvania Railroad was the dominant passenger railroad, as witnessed by the number of stations the Pennsylvania railroad built by itself or with other rail lines, beginning with Pennsylvania Station in New York City, Newark's Penn Station, Philadelphia's Broad Street and Thirtieth Street Stations, Baltimore's Penn Station, Pittsburgh's Penn Station, Union Station in Washington, D.C., and Union Station in Chicago.

ABOVE: The waiting room of the Pennsylvania Railroad Station features medallions illustrating the history of transportation, from wagons to steamships to cars and airplanes.

ABOVE: In 1968 the company merged with its long-time rival, the New York Central Railroad, forming Penn-Central Railroad. A variety of factors led to the Penn-Central Railroad filing for bankruptcy in 1971. Most of Penn Central's freight operations were placed in Conrail, the government sponsored rail corporation for the northeast. Passenger operations were taken over by state agencies, such as New Jersey Transit and MARC in Maryland, with long-distance passenger service going to Amtrak. In 1999 Norfolk Southern Railroad bought the half of Conrail containing the former Pennsylvania Railroad. The Pennsylvania Railroad is long gone but its spirit lives on in the architecturally distinguished railroad stations it left behind, including Newark's masterpiece. Pennsylvania Station was renovated in 2007 and now looks very much like it did in 1935 when it opened. It is still a major transportation hub for PATH (Port Authority Trans-Hudson), the City Subway, buses, and railroad trains.

NEWARK AIRPORT

Home to America's first major commercial airline terminal

ABOVE: Newark Airport was the first major airport in the New York metropolitan area. It was city owned and opened on October 1, 1928, on sixty-eight acres of landfill next to Port Newark. It cost $10 million to build. The combination airline terminal and administration building was opened in May, 1935, and dedicated by record-setting pilot Amelia Earhart. Before the new terminal building was opened, passengers would be split into each airline's waiting rooms. The new building helped consolidate Newark as the nation's busiest airport of the 1930s. In 1937, 270,000 passengers passed through the airport, an estimated 30 percent of all U.S. air passengers. There were so many celebrities passing through the airport that Newark's two daily newspapers devoted a column to airport comings and goings. The airport was an aviation pioneer with a number of firsts, including the first facility with paved runways, first one with instruments for landing, and first use of lights for night landings. The heaviest air traffic was between 4:30 p.m. and 6:30 p.m. each day.

RIGHT: Amelia Earhart arrives at Newark Airport after becoming the first woman to fly nonstop across the continent, as well as setting the new distance mark for female pilots.

1932

1935

ABOVE: The original art deco administration building, which included the main airline terminal (later called North Terminal) was built with WPA funds and still houses airport offices. Some have called it the most important building in U.S. aviation history because of its early consolidation of airport functions under one roof, including ticketing desks, passenger waiting room, baggage handling facilities, administrative offices, weather forecasting facilities, and an air traffic control tower. The Pulaski Skyway linking Newark Airport and Holland tunnel was built in 1932 to give quick access to the city. But New York Municipal Airport (later named LaGuardia) opened in 1939 and siphoned off much of Newark Airport's business. During Word War II the military took over Newark Airport. It became a Port of New York and New Jersey Authority airport in 1948. Over the years, EWR has expanded from the single 1935 terminal to three passenger terminals, with more than 33.7 million passengers in 2011.

LEFT: America's first commercial airline terminal, Newark featured one of the earliest air traffic control towers, a ticket counter, waiting area, airport offices, and even overnight lodging for pilots.

c.1900

PASSENGER TRAIN SERVICE
Or how the railway revolutionized traveling to and from work in New Jersey

ABOVE: In this photo, a westbound train approaches the Lackawanna Tunnel in Hoboken under Bergen Hill. The tunnel was completed in 1877 offering the DL&W Railroad its own route into Hoboken; previously it had to share a tunnel. Passenger-carrying railroads came to the state early in the nineteenth century, based on the work of Hoboken resident Colonel John Stevens, who has been called the "father of American railroading." He held the first railroad charter, was the first surveyor of a right-of-way, and the first to run a steam train. Stevens Institute of Technology is on the former Stevens family estate at Castle Point in Hoboken. His sons founded the state's first real railroad, the Camden & Amboy in 1831. By 1890 there was a growing number of people who took the train to work; factory workers rode to jobs at plants that had sprung up along railroad lines, while wealthier commuters chose to live in the New Jersey countryside and commute to the city—either Newark or New York—to work.

c.1900

ABOVE: A Delaware Lackawanna & Western Railroad train travels over a bicycle and carriage path in what is now Mount Arlington, probably on its way back from Lake Hopatcong. The railroad ran excursions from New York City (connected by ferry to Hoboken) to Lake Hopatcong.

RIGHT: The tunnel under Bergen Hill was recently refurbished by New Jersey Transit, demonstrating the importance of that hundred-year-old route in and out of Hoboken. By the first decade of the twentieth century railroads had consolidated in the state to Central Railroad of New Jersey (CNJ); Delaware, Lackawanna, and Western Railroad (DL&W); Erie Railroad; New York Central; and Pennsylvania Railroad. The building of large attractive terminals in Jersey City (CNJ) and Hoboken (DL&W) that consolidated rail and ferry boat services, coupled with the introduction of fast commuter trains, all in the first decade of the twentieth century, greatly expanded rail commuter service.

c.1905

HOBOKEN WATERFRONT
From a day trip destination for New Yorkers, to a thriving shipping center and port

LEFT: The Holland American Line docks were part of the thriving Hoboken waterfront where ocean-going freighters and transatlantic ocean liners docked, including the Hamburg America Line, North American Lloyd Line, and Holland America Line. There were also two major shipyards: Todd Shipyards and Bethlehem Steel Shipyard, along with dozens of port-related business from maritime chart sellers to ship's chandlers. Holland America's relationship with Hoboken began in 1901 when it asked permission to dredge part of the harbor so that its ships could moor there from time to time. Hoboken waterfront's first role was as a day trip destination for New Yorkers where it offered riverfront walks, picnic groves, beer gardens, and unpolluted sea air. Colonel John Stevens started the nation's first steam-powered ferry service in 1811 with the *Juliana* to bring New Yorkers to the pleasures of Hoboken. The venture ran afoul of Robert Fulton's Hudson River monopoly and didn't last. From its Elysian Fields beginning, the Hoboken waterfront evolved into a major shipping center and thriving port.

BELOW: The Holland America Line buidling on the Hoboken waterfront. The shipping company was created in Holland in 1873, starting business with only two small iron steamers. Today, it operates a fleet of twelve cruise ships calling at more than 200 ports worldwide.

c.1910

ABOVE: A fire in the abandoned buildings on Pier A—the Fifth Street pier—in the 1960s left the area derelict. By then the port was in serious decline. Elia Kazan's famous 1954 film, *On the Waterfront*, starring Marlon Brando and Karl Malden, captured the flavor of the dying waterfront in its tale of union corruption and violence on the docks. Shipping and related waterfront businesses declined as ship building became cheaper overseas, airplanes took most passenger ship traffic, and containerization reduced shipping. The Port Newark-Elizabeth Marine Terminal made city docks obsolete. The waterfront is now in the process of coming full circle back to its Elysian Fields, beginning as tree-shaded parks, with waterfront walkways lined with benches replacing decaying docks and other aspects of port life. Frank Sinatra Park, named after the legendary singer who was born in Hoboken, was created in 1998, long after the Holland America Line moved across the Hudson River to Pier 40 on Manhattan's West Side. Some miss the smell of roasting coffee after Maxwell House closed its plant in 1992.

1958

HARBOR FERRIES

A commuting ritual for many New Jersey residents until the 1960s

ABOVE: New York Central Railroad's ferryboat *Niagara*, leaving its North Shore Railroad Line pier in Weehawken in 1958. The ferryboat had been in service since 1912. Ferry service had existed for centuries between New York and New Jersey, beginning with Dutch flat-bottomed boats in the 1600s, moving to rope-towed ferries in the 1700s, to Colonel John Stevens Hoboken Ferry Company in 1821. Beginning after the Civil War, most ferries were owned by railroads in order to get their passengers from New Jersey railheads to

their jobs in New York City. The ferries' monopoly on crossing the Hudson River came to an end in 1908 when Hudson & Manhattan Railway opened, also known as "the Tube." Two years later on November 27, 1910, the Pennsylvania Railroad opened a tunnel and ran through-service under the river to its brand new Pennsylvania Station at Seventh Avenue and Thirty-fourth Street in Manhattan. Even with this competition, by 1925 ferries and trains split evenly with each carrying about 150,00 passengers daily.

c.1935

ABOVE: Railroad ferries died a slow death as passengers found other ways to get to work. In 1964, just 10,000 daily commuters used ferry service, and by 1967 ferry service had ceased. The New York Central's *Niagara* stopped running in 1959 and the same year was sold to New Jersey utility PSE&G to be used as a floating workshop, a role that lasted until 1980, when she was dismantled at Marion Generating Station in Jersey City. After a hiatus of nineteen years, trans-Hudson ferry service returned in 1986 when New York Waterway, a private company, inaugurated service from Weehawken to Pier 79 at West thirty-ninth street in Manhattan. From that single-route service developed to thirty-three boats and numerous routes, including ferries to Hoboken and Jersey City. Ferries proved invaluable after the 9/11 attacks on the World Trade Center when PATH trains to the World Trade Center site were put out of commission for almost two years.

LEFT: New York Waterway ferry *Abraham Lincoln* at its Weehawken dock, near the old operation ports of the railroad ferries.

71

HOLLAND TUNNEL

Ventilating a fume-filled tunnel provided a tricky engineering challenge for the tunnel builders

1927

ABOVE: Holland Tunnel was closed on October 29, 2012 in preparation for Hurricane Sandy. The tunnel officially reopened on November 7.

LEFT: The Holland Tunnel linking Jersey City to lower Manhattan opened on November 13, 1927, enabling cars to go from New Jersey to New York City without boarding a ferry or crossing the Hudson River in upstate New York. Construction of the $48.4 million tunnel began in 1920, with two tubes of more than 8,000 feet each. Both tubes would carry two lanes of traffic. The tunnel drilled through bedrock and at its deepest point is about ninety-three feet below "mean high water." On its first day of business 52,265 cars went through the tunnel and $26,142 was collected in tolls. Officials estimated those cars carried 200,000 persons. *The New York Times* reported in a front-page article on November 14, 1927, "A veritable wave of cars that came in the afternoon, apparently no other public work since the opening of the Brooklyn Bridge had so touched the imagination of the people."

BELOW: Holland Tunnel is essentially the same as when it was constructed except for cosmetic changes with lighting and tiles. Before the attacks of 9/11, the greatest test the tunnel faced was on May 13, 1949, when a truck explosion and fire heavily damaged 300 feet of the tunnel, destroying twenty-three trucks and injuring sixty-six people. The tunnel's ventilation system was up to the challenge that day, but maintaining fresh air in the horizontal tunnel, and removing deadly carbon monoxide gas, was a major challenge. The construction solution, after consulting mining engineers and other ventilation experts, was a unique design using eighty-four large fans and four towerlike air intake buildings, two on each side of the river to change air. Half of the fans bring in fresh air while the others work as exhaust fans. In 1984 the Holland Tunnel was designated a National Historic Civil and Mechanical Engineering Landmark for its ventilation system.

JERSEY CITY WATERFRONT

Home to the Colgate Palmolive Company until 1988

LEFT: In 1941 the Colgate Palmolive Company complex in Jersey City had grown to include offices and research laboratories as well as manufacturing facilities sprawled from Montgomery Street to Essex Street, along what is now Hudson Street. In all, it encompassed seven city blocks and forty-four buildings. Colgate had a long-time presence in Jersey City beginning in 1820 when it started up a factory here. Its first factory had been in Brooklyn, but by 1847 it had moved all manufacturing of Windsor soap and Pearl Starch, its main products, to Jersey City. The iconic Colgate clock, facing New York harbor, was placed on top of the manufacturing building in 1908. Its octagon shape was designed as an advertisement for one of Colgate's important products, Octagon Soap. It was replaced in 1924 by the present clock, which is 50 feet in diameter with a minute hand weighing 2,200 pounds. Jersey City's indomitable Mayor, Frank Hague, was at the clock's dedication ceremony and set the monster clock in motion. At that time it was considered the largest clock in the world.

ABOVE: Goldman Sachs Tower, completed in 2004, stands at the southern end of the former Colgate property with the clock (viewed side-on here) at its base. It is the tallest building in New Jersey, and some architectural critics have said it has more in common with skyscrapers across the river in Manhattan than it does with its surroundings in Jersey City. The forty-two-story tower was designed by well-known architect Cesar Pelli, who designed the World Finance Center buildings next to the World Trade Center site; the Petronas Tower in Kuala Lumpur, Malaysia; One Canada Square in the Docklands section of London; and Key Tower in Cleveland. The Colgate buildings were demolished in 1988 following Colgate's abandonment of Jersey City in 1985.

LEFT: When the clock was stopped at 9:30 a.m. on June 13, 1955, for repairs, the company received hundreds of calls by those counting on the clock to keep them on schedule. Such reaction bears testimony to the clock's practicality and identity as a symbol of the Colgate company.

1892

ELLIS ISLAND
Symbol of American immigration and the immigrant experience

ABOVE: Immigration facilities on Ellis Island processed the ancestors of more than 100 million Americans living today. The facility was open from January 1, 1892, until it closed in 1954. The main building dates from 1900 and is a French Renaissance style designed by New York City architects William Boring and Edward Tilton. It was erected following a fire in 1897 that destroyed the existing wooden building. During the sixty-two years of its working life, more than 12 million immigrants took their first steps towards becoming Americans here. The peak of Ellis Island's role as the main U.S. immigration depot was from 1892 until 1920; after that, would-be immigrants were examined in U.S. consulates abroad. The busiest day on record was April 17, 1907, when 11,274 people were processed. It was mostly poor people who had to endure the long lines, medical checks, and questions. First- and second-class passengers, who were immigrants on the same ships, were generally screened onboard.

RIGHT: The Registry Hall, centerpiece of the immigration examining process, was on the second floor of the main building up a long staircase. If would-be immigrants had difficulty climbing the stairs or looked unduly fatigued they were pulled out of line for a physical examination. Once in the Registry Hall, people were quizzed about a number of things. Included among the twenty-nine questions were: name, home town, occupation, destination, and amount of money. Only 2 percent of potential immigrants were denied entry.

c.1905

c.1905

ABOVE: After closing in 1954, the island fell into decay. It was made part of the Statue of Liberty National Monument in 1965 and first opened to the public a decade later. The decaying main immigration depot was only revitalized by a citizens committee led by Lee Iacocca, then Chairman of Chrysler Corporation, who raised $600 million from corporations and ordinary Americans to rehabilitate both Ellis Island and the Statue of Liberty. After a six-year renovation, the main building reopened in 1990 and now is home to the Ellis Island Immigration Museum, which features rooms restored to their early 1900s look, including the Registry Hall, the centerpiece of an immigrant's experience on the island.

The jurisdiction of Ellis Island has been a long, drawn-out controversy between New Jersey and New York. Glancing at a nautical chart one can readily see that Ellis Island is part of Jersey City, but it took a 1998 U.S. Supreme Court decision—*New Jersey versus New York*, case number 120—to establish that fact.

ABOVE LEFT AND LEFT: New arrivals at Ellis Island disembark from ferries, brought over from the passenger liners docked in New York harbor. There would invariably be a long wait on benches in the open air when weather was good to see immigration officials.

77

1939

JOURNAL SQUARE, JERSEY CITY
Location of Jersey City's first skyscraper, the Labor Bank Building

ABOVE: Journal Square, in April 1939, was the hub of Jersey City. The square is named after the *Jersey Journal*, a Newhouse newspaper that has long been a Hudson County staple. Billboards reflect long-gone products such as Ballantine Ale, a major sponsor of the New York Yankees baseball team, and Sinclair gasoline. In the distance is the 200-foot bell and clock tower of John the Baptist Roman Catholic Church on Hudson Boulevard. The Journal Square area began to develop in 1912 after the Hudson & Manhattan Railroad—"the Tube"—

opened its Summit Avenue station there, but the square itself dates from 1923 when the *Jersey Journal* offices were demolished allowing a broad intersection with Hudson Boulevard and Bergen Street. The city's first skyscraper was built at the newly-formed square in 1928, the fifteen-story Labor Bank Building at 26 Journal Square (not shown). The square had three major ornate movie theaters, Loew's, built in 1929; Stanley, built in 1928; and State, built in 1922.

ABOVE: Journal Square is dominated by the ten-story Port of New York & New Jersey Authority building that includes a combination PATH station and bus depot. It opened in stages between 1974–1975 at a cost of $126 million. Critics have argued the cost was far greater in human terms as the transportation center led to the decline of Journal Square. By moving bus stops and PATH stations, pedestrians (potential shoppers) were shifted away from stores and other businesses. The building, housing PATH system headquarters, is built over the Bergen Hill Cut, a famous Pennsylvania Railroad passage through the Palisades to the Jersey City waterfront. The nine-story gray building next to Port Authority Building is an office building erected in 1987. Hudson County Community College has several buildings around the square. There are a number of plans for high-rise development but nothing has been built recently. The intersection of Hudson Boulevard (renamed Kennedy Boulevard) and Bergen Street still form the top of the square; the clock tower of John the Baptist Roman Catholic Church is still visible.

c.1938

JERSEY CITY MEDICAL CENTER
The project of mayor Frank Hague who had a secret office at the complex

LEFT: A hospital has been at the site of the sprawling Jersey City Medical Center at Baldwin Avenue and Montgomery Street since 1881. The facility was another project of Jersey City's long-time dictatorial mayor Frank Hague. Construction began in 1928 and lasted until 1941. The complex contained about a dozen buildings, including ten- and fourteen-story high-rises made of a pale yellow brick with terra-cotta designs. Most buildings are the work of Architect John T. Rowland and many were put up by the Depression-era Works Progress Administration. Jersey City had more WPA projects than any other New Jersey city. The facility had lavish marble interiors with terrazzo floors, fancy moldings, and other touches one wouldn't expect in a hospital. Mayor Hague had a secret office at the complex. Franklin Roosevelt dedicated the B. S. Pollack Hospital, one of the key components of the medical center, on October 2, 1936. The medical complex was also famous for its Margaret Hague Maternity Hospital, named after Mayor Hague's mother.

ABOVE: From the very beginning the medical complex was far too large for the community it served. Some have estimated that it was three times the size needed, and from the start had financial difficulties. Various attempts were made to make the complex a success, such as housing Seton Hall University's medical and dental school there from 1954 to 1964. The medical school was sold to the state in 1965 and became New Jersey College of Medicine and Dentistry. The Jersey City Medical Complex closed in 1988. It had become too big and too expensive and was understaffed and underutilized. The medical center name is still used for a privately run hospital, relocated in 2004 to smaller quarters at Grand Street and Jersey Avenue downtown. The former medical center site is being developed into the Beacon complex, a mixed-use development of apartments and stores. The complex sits on a ridge of the Palisades, the highest point in Jersey City, giving it a commanding view of over the rest of Jersey City and into Manhattan.

c.1940

ROOSEVELT STADIUM / DROYER'S POINT

Jackie Robinson (whose middle name was Roosevelt) made his minor league debut here in 1946

ABOVE: Roosevelt Stadium was created to bring professional sports and concerts to Jersey City. It was built with $1.5 million of WPA funds, opening on April 23, 1937. The 24,000-seat stadium was designed by Christian H. Ziegler on the former Jersey City Airport site at Droyer's Point, adjacent to what is now Route 440. It was a pet project of Mayor "I am the law" Frank Hague, Jersey City's mayor of thirty years and the Hudson County political boss. He was mayor of Jersey City from 1917 to 1947 and vice-chairman of the Democratic Party National Committee from 1924 to 1949. The stadium was important in breaking down racial barriers. Jackie Robinson—the first African American to play major league baseball—made his debut here on April 18, 1946 in a minor league game between the Jersey City Giants and Montreal Royals. The Giants lost 14–1, although Robinson hit a home run. The Jersey City Giants, an international league affiliate of the New York Giants, was based here from 1937 to 1950.

1956

ABOVE: Throughout its history, the stadium was more than simply a sports stadium. It served as a gathering place for sports—mostly high school sports—but also as a venue for concerts, marching band competitions, and school graduations. It fell into disuse in the late 1970s because it cost more to maintain the facility than the incoming revenue warranted. It was demolished in 1985. On the verge of the stadium's demolition, *The New York Times* called it a "paradigm of elegance in a blue-collar town." It was replaced by the gated community of Society Hill, which had a groundbreaking ceremony in 1989 but most construction didn't take place until the mid-1990s. Building was delayed because of chromium-contaminated soil in a section of the complex that had to be abated. The heavy-metal pollution was blamed on earlier manufacturing plants in the area.

LEFT: The Brooklyn Dodgers played fifteen home games at Roosevelt Stadium in 1956 as the team contemplated its move away from Ebbets Field.

1893

1924

ABOVE: The station at Elizabeth is one of the few examples of Richardson Romanesque railroad architecture to survive pretty much as it was designed.

BELOW: A postcard view from 1910.

ELIZABETH RAILROAD STATION
From station linking the Pennsylvania Railroad to the Central Railroad of New Jersey, to quirky restaurant

ABOVE: The impressive stone and brick Central Railroad of New Jersey station at Broad Street in Elizabeth was built between 1891 and 1892 at a cost of $38,000. It was designed by architect Bruce Price in a modified Richardson Romanesque style. The use of columns instead of arches to frame the windows and the use of lighter-colored brick gives the station an open feeling. (A footnote about Price: he was the father of famed etiquette advice giver Emily Post.) The tower had a hand-wound clock that was used until the station closed. It was one of the few stations where the tracks of the Pennsylvania Railroad and the Central Railroad of New Jersey (also called Jersey Central Railroad) crossed, allowing passengers access to both systems. The CNJ railroad started life as the Elizabeth & Somerville Railroad in 1838 and the Somerville and Easton Railroad, founded in 1847. The two railroads combined and gradually merged with or acquired others to become the Central Railroad of New Jersey in 1849.

ABOVE: The Central Railroad of New Jersey (CNJ) Station in Elizabeth is now a restaurant. In its last days it served as the headquarters for the CNJ medical department. All rail service was shifted to the former Pennsylvania railroad tracks about 50 yards from the old CNJ right-of-way and station in the late 1970s. The station was active from 1893 to 1978. The CNJ underwent a long decline beginning with its filing for bankruptcy in 1939. After reorganization it still faced problems and disappeared forever on April 1, 1976, when it became part of the federally owned Consolidated Rail Corporation, also known as Conrail. A number of proposals for developing downtown Elizabeth, and separate New Jersey Transit proposals, could have an impact on the historic Elizabeth train station. One proposal would use the old station as a drop-off point for commuters known as "Kiss and Ride." Another would make the station a bus stop on a proposed Bus Rapid Transit system that would use the former CNJ right-of-way (see right).

1953

NEW JERSEY TURNPIKE
The first sections opened in 1951 to alleviate traffic in central and northern New Jersey

LEFT: The Secaucus toll booth in 1953, shortly after the 118-mile New Jersey Turnpike opened on January 15, 1952. It cost $255 million and took two years and one month to build. The Turnpike had its precursor in two proposed 1930s roads, Routes 100 and 300. Traffic had become so snarled along busy U.S. Route 1 corridor in central and northern New Jersey, and U.S. Route 130 corridor in southern New Jersey, that something had to be done to alleviate congestion. New Jersey Department of Transportation did not have money for projects in the Depression-era 1930s and then World War II further limited road-building money. Very little of these two roadways were actually built. In 1948 New Jersey legislature created New Jersey Turnpike Authority to build the crucial link between New York and Philadelphia. Governor Alfred Driscoll, who was a strong proponent of the roadway, wanted the best and safest highway in the country. He hired General W. W. Wanamaker, a retired Army Corps of Engineers officer as first executive director.

ABOVE: The sign was advertising the turnpike to prospective customers taking the rail line that ran just to the left in the picture.

ABOVE: Secaucus tollbooth has expanded dramatically since its opening, just like the Turnpike itself. The Turnpike was widened and extended over the years, with extensions to the Holland Tunnel and Pennsylvania Turnpike, to name two. The Turnpike is now 148 miles of roadway with as many as fourteen lanes at some points, a big jump from its initial four lanes. But its early highway innovations survived the test of time—such as twelve-foot-wide vehicle lanes (compared to the traditional ten feet), limited and controlled access to the roadway, with 1,200-foot-long entry and exit lanes. Other innovations included clear signage, highway curves, and graded elevations. The turnpike has twelve rest areas, named after prominent people with ties to New Jersey, such as Walt Whitman, and presidents Grover Cleveland and Woodrow Wilson, as well as football coach Vince Lombardi, who once coached in the state. In 2010, 236.8 million vehicles used the roadway, less than the 384.1 million vehicles that used the Garden State Parkway in the same period.

LEFT: This photograph shows cars heading towards Linden using the New Jersey Turnpike and the prominent New Jersey landmark, the former Esso refinery, in the background.

1936

6-341

ROYAL GOVERNOR'S MANSION, PERTH AMBOY

Residence of the last British Royal Governor, William Franklin, son of Benjamin Franklin

LEFT: The nation's only standing colonial royal governor's mansion was in good condition at the time of this picture in 1936. It was built between 1768 and 1770 in what was called the British Palladian style. It was a two-story masonry building made from bricks brought over from England, probably as ship's ballast as Perth Amboy is a port city (the third story to the house would be added in 1808). In 1686 Perth Amboy was made the capital of East Jersey and it was home to the offices of the East Jersey Proprietors' Association, owners of vast tracts of land in what is now central and northern New Jersey. The house was erected by Proprietors of East Jersey as the official residence for Royal Governors of New Jersey. William Franklin, the son of patriot Benjamin Franklin, was the last Royal Governor. He lived in the house briefly from October 1774 to 1775 when he was placed under house arrest by revolutionaries. He later left for New York City and after the war moved to London.

ABOVE: The house at 149 Kearny Avenue in Perth Amboy underwent a variety of uses over the years, ranging from a pensioner's home, to a hotel, to a rooming house. The state bought the property in 1967. It is run and maintained by the nonprofit Proprietary House Association. It was placed on the National Register of Historic Places in 1971. In 1998 the East Jersey Proprietors, then New Jersey's oldest corporation, disbanded and sold their "rights to unappropriated land" to the state's Green Acres program. The role of proprietors in the life of the Colony of East Jersey (most of north and central New Jersey) led to three centuries of legal battles over deeds and ownership of land issues. The last legal questions were finally resolved in the waning days of the twentieth century, but it had been a legal nightmare akin to *Jarndyce vs. Jarndyce* in Charles Dickens' masterful novel, *Bleak House*. The West Jersey Proprietors'—based in Burlington—claims were settled long ago. The state archives now has the records from both East and West Jersey.

1909

RUTGERS FOOTBALL
The first American university student football team

ABOVE: The first college football game took place November 6, 1869, between Rutgers University and Princeton on the Rutgers campus in New Brunswick. Each team fielded twenty-five players in a game more like rugby than modern football, with Rutgers winning. Scoring was like that in tennis with a series of games making a match. The 1909 photo shows Rutgers playing Haverford with uniforms much like the original ones, the major difference was that no helmet or padding was worn in the original game. The Rutgers student newspaper, *The Targum* (now *Daily Targum*), reporting in 1869 wrote, "… every game was like the one before. There was the same headlong running wild, shouting, and frantic kicking. In every game the cool goaltenders saved the Rutgers goal half a dozen times, in every game the heavy charger of the Princeton side overthrew everything he came in contact with." Rutgers won games 1, 3, 5, 6, 9, and 10, winning the match.

1909

ABOVE: Football at Rutgers University has evolved from that first game played on a dirt and grass field (now buried beneath the College Avenue gymnasium) to a 52,454-seat stadium and two practice fields. Rutgers football had a fairly consistent schedule from its first game until the late 1960s, playing mainly Ivy League schools, and smaller colleges like Haverford, Colgate, and Army, with an occasional Notre Dame or Alabama mixed in. Beginning in the late 1970s, Rutgers began playing mostly powerful football schools like

Syracuse and Tulane. In 1991 Rutgers joined the Big East Conference, which was followed by a decade-long slump and a rebuilding of their program beginning in 2001 under then coach Greg Schiano. Since 2002 Rutgers has won sixty-six games, lost fifty-one, and played in five bowl games (in late 2012 Rutgers joined the Big Ten Football Conference). The late Alabama University Coach, Bear Bryant, said before a game with Rutgers in 1979, "That's where football started, so if it weren't for Rutgers I wouldn't have a job." A statue on Scarlet Walk into Rutgers stadium pays tribute to that first game.

LEFT AND ABOVE LEFT: Football game between Rutgers University and Haverford College.

1948

PRINCETON UNIVERSITY

Fourth-oldest college in the United States and world-renowned research center

ABOVE: The Gothic spires of the Princeton University Chapel highlight the school's genesis as an institution to educate Presbyterian clergy. The chapel was designed by Ralph Adams Clam who was the university's chief architect from 1907 to 1929. The state's premier university, the fourth chartered of nine colonial colleges, and New Jersey's contribution to the Ivy League, was founded in Elizabeth in 1747 as the College of New Jersey (no relation to former Trenton State College that poached the name). The school later moved to Newark holding its first commencement on November 9, 1748, under its new president Reverend Aaron Burr, father of future Vice-President Aaron Burr Jr. The college moved to Princeton—favored by the trustees because it was halfway between New York and Philadelphia—in 1756 into the newly completed Nassau Hall. On October 22, 1896, the university changed its name to Princeton University. Part of the Revolutionary War Battle of Princeton, on January 2–3, 1777, took place on the university campus at Nassau Hall.

1903

1942

FAR LEFT: Soldiers march past Blair Hall, on their way to class during an Army Specialist Training Program. Running since 1919, Princeton army courses embody the university's motto, "In the Nation's Service, and In the Service of All Nations."

LEFT: Blair Hall, the University's first collegiate Gothic dormitory, was a Sesquicentennial gift of John Insley Blair (1802–1899), a trustee of Princeton from 1866 to 1899. Blair Hall and its south section, Buyers Hall, were renovated in 2000 as part of Princeton's thirty-year plan to renovate every undergraduate dormitory.

RIGHT: Princeton University's 500-acre campus has an eclectic mix of buildings and architectural styles. The chapel today is still one of the university's most prominent buildings and remains unaltered from its 1928 dedication. It is made of Pennsylvania sandstone, with highly decorative carved ornamentals and a number of stained glass windows. University alumni are as distinguished as its campus architecture. They include two U.S. presidents—James Madison and Woodrow Wilson—nine founding fathers, forty governors, more than 200 congressmen, and twenty-two Nobel prize winners. U.S. President Woodrow Wilson was also president of Princeton University from 1902 to 1910. The university has 5,000 undergraduate students today in thirty-four academic departments. The university has no medical, business, or law school, but does offer graduate degrees in architecture and engineering. The other university dating from colonial days is Rutgers, the state university, founded by the Dutch Reformed Church as Queens College in 1766 to educate clergy.

LEFT: The U.S. Department of the Interior designated Nassau Hall a National Historic Landmark in 1960.

1893

TRENTON BATTLE MONUMENT

Commemorating a pivotal victory for the Continental forces during the American Revolutionary War

LEFT: The Trenton Battle Monument, at its dedication ceremony in 1893, located on a slight hill above downtown Trenton. The monument marks the spot where Colonel Henry Knox placed his artillery during the Battle of Trenton on December 26, 1777. The area is known as Five Points because five major roads intersect and artillery placed there could dominate the city. The monument was designed by John H. Duncan, who also planned Grant's Tomb in New York City. It consists of a triangular base, with bronze plaques depicting battle scenes, and a 135-foot Doric column with a golden-color statue of George Washington on top. Guarding the entrance to the monument are two bronze statues of Continental soldiers, looking more like citizens of the republic than part of a uniformed militia.

ABOVE: The bronze plaques showing battle scenes, by Thomas Eakins, are refitted in 1969.

RIGHT: The monument has an elevator inside to take people up to view a panorama of Trenton, but the state park has been closed since 2010. Apart from the bronze plaques depicting battle scenes there is also a plaque of Washington crossing the Delaware, reminding us that his plan called for three separate crossings and that ice and heavy snow storms kept the other divisions from crossing. The battle was a major turning point in the American Revolution.

c.1970

NEW JERSEY STATE HOUSE, TRENTON
Home to New Jersey's Senate and General Assembly since 1792

LEFT: The State House was designed for the Senate, General Assembly, and governor's office to be all under one roof. The original building of 1792 was designed by Jonathan Doane and parts are still visible in the Governor's office wing. The building of today, with a three-story classical façade of granite columns and rotunda topped by a gilded dome, dates from 1895. The State House was reconstructed following a March 21, 1885, fire that destroyed much of the front of the building. The French Renaissance façade was designed by Lewis H. Broome, who also designed City Hall in Jersey City.

BELOW: A ground level view of the second State House, on West State Street, in the 1930s.

c.1930

ABOVE AND BELOW: The exterior of the State House hasn't changed since its 1898 reconstruction, but the site has evolved into a Capitol Complex. It has steadily expanded from the 1920s when the State House Annex was added, initially for courts, now used as legislative hearing rooms. In the 1960s, the state library and museum buildings were added, considerably expanding the Capitol complex. In the mid-1990s a legislative staff building and new visitor center were built and an underground parking garage was constructed. Much earlier, interior spaces in the State House were renovated. The Senate Chambers were redone in 1905 in the American Renaissance style by Merchantville architect Arnold Moses. The Assembly has eighty members while the Senate has forty members; all legislators are elected from forty districts throughout the state, each one containing the same population as per a state Supreme Court order. Assemblymen and women serve two-year terms, while state senators serve four-year terms.

1893

TRENTON STREETSCAPE

Downtown Trenton has been buzzing with commercial activities since the 1890s

LEFT: The downtown business district of Trenton as it looked in 1893, at the intersection of State and Warren streets. The business district was centered on State Street and the several blocks intersecting it, North Warren, Broad, and Montgomery streets. On the corner, at 2–4 North Warren Street was the Western Union Telegraph office, with a dentist's office on the second floor. Next door, at Number 6, was a drugstore and at Number 8, a jewelry store. The buildings were erected in 1833 as part of a commercial development scheme of Armitage Green with stores on the ground level and offices on other floors. The storefronts were modernized sometime in the early 1890s. The taller, narrow building at Number 10 was built in 1887 by Albert Smith as a four-story commercial building. Smith's first tenant was Claffery & Slack Co., which sold saddles and related equestrian items as well as carriage hardware.

RIGHT: The intersection of West State and North Warren streets continues today as the commercial hub of downtown Trenton. Stores and buildings there have changed over the years reflecting technological and preference shifts, but interestingly, there was a tobacco shop at 2 North Warren Street from 1895 to 1987, the last one was Webster Cigars. The last occupants of stores at 4 to 8 North Warren Street include Hoagle Hamlet, selling subs and salads; a Rexall Drugstore at 10, and a store called Tempo at 8. The building at Number 10, more distinctive architecturally than its neighbors, was a long-time drugstore after the saddle business folded. All the buildings on the first block of North Warren Street were torn down in September 1987 to make way for a six-story office building with a TD Bank branch on the ground floor. The intersection has been a popular location from the 1830s into the twenty-first century because it is two blocks from the State House and a similar distance from City Hall.

1908

ROEBLING PLANT, TRENTON
A leading steel manufacturer who supplied cables for America's greatest bridges

ABOVE: John A. Roebling's Sons Company on Hamilton Avenue and surrounding streets was a major steel wire producer and one of the city's most important industries. There had been a Roebling factory in Trenton since 1856. In 1901 the Roebling plant employed 2,250 people. Roebling's specialty was making wire cables for suspension bridges, and later steel wire for precast concrete bridges. The Brooklyn Bridge, completed in 1883, was the project that made the Roebling company known worldwide. The bridge was the first suspension bridge to use steel cable instead of wrought iron. The cables were made from spun wire by using John Roebling's patented spinning wheel system on the site. In the 1890s cable to pull streetcars was a growing market that Roebling dominated. Streetcars needed long wire rope without splices. Roebling invented a machine to make up to 30,000 feet of 1.5-inch wire rope, called "the Eighty Ton Wire Rope Machine."

c.1900

ABOVE: About half of the Roebling mill complex, including all of its signature tall smokestacks, have been torn down. Other parts of the sprawling complex are being recycled into offices, a shopping center, and cultural spaces. Perhaps sensing a changing steel industry, the Roebling family sold the company in 1953 to CFI Steel. Roebling's two main products, wire cable and steel wire for prestressed concrete bridges, were both losing sales. The former because of changing bridge technologies and the latter because of intense competition from other producers who entered the market when interstate highway construction began. CFI closed the factory in 1973 citing low profits and inefficiency. Before its demise, the company had furnished wire cable for some of the country's iconic bridges including the George Washington Bridge and the Golden Gate Bridge. It was Roebling, Goodyear, Lenox, and other manufacturers that gave substance to the city's motto, "Trenton Makes, the World Takes." It is still displayed on the Warren Street Bridge, confusing people who only think of Trenton as the state capital.

LEFT: The Roebling's Sons Company and American Steel & Wire Company plant which stretched over South Broad, Clark, Elmer, Mott & Hudson streets in Trenton.

1938

CRANBERRY HARVESTING

New Jersey was America's major producer of cranberries until the early twentieth century

ABOVE: Cranberry harvesting as it was practiced in October 1938, in Burlington County in the Pine Barrens. Around that time the state was the number one cranberry producer in the country. In 1936 the state had 9,500 acres of cranberries under cultivation. The most important counties were Burlington, Ocean, and Atlantic. Cranberries are a native New Jersey plant found in the wild here and one of only three major fruits native to North America. The Pine Barrens provides ideal growing conditions in New Jersey's little-known wilderness with its stunted trees and sandy acidic soils. Man-made bogs for harvesting the cranberries have been used since the first bog in 1835. This wet method is used as a New Jersey Agricultural Experiment Station booklet explained, "Cranberries do not grow in the water. Cranberries grow on low-lying vines in sandy soil that are flooded for wet harvesting in the fall, then reflooded for the duration of winter to protect plants from cold-weather damage."

1938

ABOVE: Cranberries are still among the state's top ten agricultural products while nationally the state ranks third in producing them, behind Wisconsin and Massachusetts. For the nineteenth and early twentieth centuries, New Jersey was the premier cranberry producer, but false blossom disease severely affected the crop in the early 1910s and production hasn't been in first place since then. Harvest at Haines & Haines, the state's largest producer, with 1,400 acres in production, takes place each year from late September to mid-October. The family farm has third-, fourth-, and fifth-generation family members working in the operation. Most of the cranberry crop goes to Ocean Spray—a grower's cooperative founded by farmers from New Jersey, Massachusetts, and Wisconsin. Cranberries are harvested by a machine that looks like a giant lawnmower with attached beaters below the water's surface that knock the cranberries from their vines. The berries, which are hollow in the center, become buoyant rising to the surface where they are gathered.

LEFT: Cranberry cultivation is believed to have begun in 1840, when John Webb established a cranberry bog in Ocean County. His cranberries were bought by whalers who kept the fruits on board ships in barrels of cold water to prevent scurvy.

BATSTO MANSION, PINE BARRENS

Former residence of generations of ironmasters, the mansion reflects the prosperity enjoyed during Batsto's industrial years

c.1910

c.1955

BELOW: Joseph Wharton, owner of Batsto Village, died in 1909 leaving his various farming enterprises to be managed by Girard Trust Co. of Philadelphia until 1954 when the state bought the property. Land bought by the state formed the core of Wharton State Forest's 110,000 acres. The forest protects one of the largest aquifers in the East.

The name Batsto comes from the Swedish word Batstu meaning bathing place—it bordered the river—now the Batsto River. Swedes settled in various parts of the West Jersey Colony. Tucked away in that mysterious part of New Jersey, a sprawling semi-wilderness with few people, home to the Jersey Devil and the cranberry industry, Batsto suffered a slow decline from a population of 280 in 1900 to the last family leaving there in 1989.

LEFT: The Batsto mansion was built in 1826 and extensively remodeled in the 1870s in an Italianate style. The home, once also known as the Richards Mansion, was the center of Batsto village life. The iron works founded by Charles Read of Burlington in 1766, was a supplier of cannon balls, camp kettles, iron fastenings, and other iron products to the Continental Army. The burgeoning industrial complex in the Pinelands was sold in 1784 to William Richards, whose family ran the iron works and later a glass factory until 1876. Most of the village buildings and sawmill date from their ownership. The bog iron industry declined because of increased competition from iron ore and by 1855 it had ceased at Batsto. The complex then shifted to glass manufacturing, which also declined. The industrial village, which included 50,000 acres of surrounding forests and farms, was sold at auction in 1876 to financier Joseph Wharton of Philadelphia. He tried farming various products with limited success.

ABOVE: Batsto Village is located near a river and a lake, which favored the iron industry. The river was a source for bog ore, and the lake, created by the dam, allowed boats to move bog iron from rivers and streams to the iron furnace. The lake also provided water power for the sawmill and gristmill.

1936

INDIAN KING TAVERN, HADDONFIELD
Where New Jersey officially became a state in 1777

LEFT: The General Assembly met at the Indian King Tavern on September 20, 1777 and unanimously resolved that "thereafter the word state should be substituted for colony in all public writs and commissions." Earlier that year, in May, the tavern was the place where the state's official seal was adopted and also a Council of Safety was created to defend the Revolution against residents who supported the British. The tavern, built in 1750 and later enlarged, was made of brick and stucco. It is considered a fine example of eighteenth-century tavern architecture. The tavern was the site of many important meetings because its second floor hall was the largest nonreligious meeting space in New Jersey at the time. The Indian King Tavern takes its name from another defunct tavern that was built in Haddonfield in the mid-1750s, named Indian King after the Lenni Lenape Indian chiefs whose tribes once occupied the area.

ABOVE: The Indian King Tavern, Haddonfield, has been administered by the state since 1903 and listed on the National Register of Historic Places from 1970. Perhaps one of the lasting legacies of the Indian King isn't that it is a fine example of eighteenth-century tavern architecture, but it is the intangible one of hosting important meetings in the early days of the state. Meetings were held here because warfare in central New Jersey made meetings in Trenton impossible. The seal, which is still in use today with some minor alterations, was designed by Pierre Eugene du Simitiere, a Swiss-born artist who also designed the state seals of Virginia, Delaware, and Georgia.

c.1930

WALT WHITMAN HOUSE

Museum commemorating the life of the author of *Leaves of Grass*

LEFT: *Oh Captain, My Captain!* is probably Walt Whitman's most famous poem, one that pays tribute to an assassinated President Abraham Lincoln. Whitman wrote the poem in 1865 when his mother was already living in Camden, New Jersey. Whitman himself lived in Camden from 1873 until his death in March 26, 1892. He bought the house at 328 Mickle Boulevard, shown here in the mid-1930s, in 1884 for $1,750. The house was built in 1848 and was the only house he ever owned. In the last years of his life he designed his own tomb for his burial at nearby Harlerigh Cemetery.

ABOVE RIGHT: Walt Whitman with his nurse on a wharf near his house. The poet has been declared America's first "poet of democracy." Whitman's vagabond lifestyle was adopted by the Beat movement, and in particular Allen Ginsberg and Jack Kerouac in the 1950s and early 1960s.

1890

RIGHT: The Walt Whitman House became a state historic site by a circuitous route. After Whitman's death, his heirs rented out the property, which had fallen into disrepair. The city of Camden bought the house in 1921 and five years later opened it as a house museum. In 1947 the state took over the house, most of Whitman's contents remained. The house was listed on the National Register of Historic Places in 1966 and made a National Historic Landmark in 1978. The house has been restored and furnished to look as it did in the last years Whitman lived there, including his second-floor retreat that he called his den, filled with books and pictures. The house features some original furnishings and Whitman memorabilia. Whitman is best known for his volume of poetry "Leaves of Grass," but he was also a journalist and essayist, a volunteer nurse in Washington, D.C., during the Civil War, and for a time a government clerk. He is considered the father of free verse poetry and one of America's greatest poets.

1969

THE BATTLESHIP NEW JERSEY
A ship that saw service in three very different theaters of war

LEFT: The USS *New Jersey* in action off the central Vietnam coast in late-March 1969. She was built in the Philadelphia Naval Shipyard and launched in 1943. When she was launched, the ship—designated BB-62—was 887 feet long, 108 feet wide, and displaced 58,000 tons of water, with a top speed of 33 knots. She had nine batteries of 16-inch guns that could fire a 2,700 pound shell 23 miles. She had a crew of 151 officers and 2,637 enlisted sailors. She was the second battleship named *New Jersey*. The first Battleship *New Jersey*, designated BB-16, was launched November 10, 1904, from the Fore River Ship Building Company in Quincy, Massachusetts. She was a Virginia-class battleship that was part of the Great White Fleet that sailed around the world as a demonstration of American naval power from December 1907 to February 1909. She was decommissioned in August 1920 and was sunk off North Carolina in a famous bombing test conducted by Army Brigadier General Billy Mitchell in 1923.

1915

ABOVE & BELOW: *New Jersey* conducted regular operations along the east coast and in the Caribbean until the outbreak of World War I.

1909

ABOVE: The most decorated ship in U.S. Naval history, the USS *New Jersey*, also affectionately called "the Big J," is tethered to its Delaware River dock in Camden. She is now a floating museum after seeing action in World War II, the Korean War, Vietnam, and off Lebanon in 1983. During that long stretch of service the ship had only one fatality, which happened during the Korean War when a shore battery made a direct hit. She was awarded nineteen battle and campaign stars for her actions in the three major conflicts. The ship had been decommissioned and then recommissioned three times; its fourth and final decommissioning took place in February 1991. The ship was towed from its reserve fleet anchorage in Bremerton, Washington, to its new owners in Camden in September 1999. The nonprofit organization that owns the ship wants to restore it to its 1990 condition. It opened for public visits in October 2001.

1916

SUMMER WHITEHOUSE

From residence of retail magnate Hubert Parson, to Monmouth University building

ABOVE: Shadow Lawn was President Woodrow Wilson's summer residence in West Long Branch. It was where he received notification that the Democratic Party had nominated him to be its candidate for president in 1912. Prior to the 1932 Democratic convention, when Franklin D. Roosevelt was nominated, candidates didn't attend their party's convention but were notified of the results. The house, which President Wilson went on to call his "summer White House," was built in 1902 by James Carly at a cost of $500,000 for Joseph McCall, President of New York Life

Insurance Co. The house had thirty-two well-appointed rooms. The original house burned down on January 8, 1927, and the Associated Press reported it, "a huge heap of smoldering timber remained today of Shadow Lawn show place of New Jersey and summer White House during the administration of President Woodrow Wilson." The owner of the mansion at the time was Hubert Parson, president of F. W. Woolworth. He bought the house in 1918 from New York department store magnate G. B. Greenhut, who loaned the house to Wilson.

1916

ABOVE: The mansion on the campus of Monmouth University is sometimes called Shadow Lawn, but its correct name is Woodrow Wilson Hall, itself an important building that is listed on the National Register of Historic Places.

LEFT: Woodrow Wilson used Shadow Lawn to entertain, but it was owned by a New York retail magnate.

It was built in 1929 at a cost of $10.5 million to replace the original Shadow Lawn mansion that burned down. Philadelphia architect Horace Trumbauer and his assistant Julian Abele, the first African-American architect, designed the mansion in neoclassical French style for Hubert T. Parsons, president of the F. W. Woolworth Company, the mansion's owner. To confuse matters further, Parsons still called his new home Shadow Lawn.

The mansion had 130 rooms including nineteen bathrooms. Its exterior is clad with limestone and is on the same site as the original Shadow Lawn. The university uses the building as a conference center and for special functions. It became part of Monmouth University in 1956. In 1982 it was used as the home of Daddy Warbucks in the movie *Annie*. It was made a National Historic Landmark on February 2, 1985.

1903

ASBURY PARK
Named for the first Methodist bishop in the United States

ABOVE: Asbury Park was a fashionable resort in 1903 and Lake Wesley a popular spot for boating and relaxing. The lake is named after John Wesley, the founder of Methodism. It divides Asbury Park from Ocean Grove, a Methodist camp meeting settlement. The man-made lake is encircled by concrete retaining walls. Paddle boats, some shaped like swans, were a feature of the lake from the late 1800s until the early 1970s when Asbury Park fell on hard times. The seaside town was created as a resort by New York businessman James A. Bradley, a brush manufacturer. The city is named after Francis Asbury, the first Methodist bishop in the United States. Bradley created the

boardwalk, public bathhouses for changing, and other facilities that in turn attracted other businessmen who installed amusements along the boardwalk. The city has had several periods of popularity, and during its first period in the 1890s, it attracted more than 600,000 summer visitors who came to the shore by train from New York City and Philadelphia.

RIGHT: Boating was not the only activity to be enjoyed in Asbury Park; there was also the Tillie Palace Amusements, opened in 1888. The park featured a sixty-seven-foot-high wheel that gave passengers unparalleled views of Asbury Park, Ocean Grove, and the Atlantic Ocean. The park, with its iconic wall murals showing Tillie's grinning face, was razed in 2004.

1901

ABOVE: Swan boats have returned to Wesley Lake, perhaps one of the more visible signs of Asbury Park's rebound after decades in the doldrums. Asbury Park was a popular destination from the 1920s to the 1940s, but it began to lose visitors in the 1950s with the opening of the Garden State Parkway. Summer visitors no longer took trains to the shore but drove to other beachfront towns. Many residents moved to surrounding suburbs as farmland gave way to housing developments and area shopping malls siphoned business from downtown stores. Riots broke out in Asbury Park on July 4, 1970, resulting in widespread property damage and some sections have not been redeveloped to this day. In 1973 Bruce Springsteen released his first album, *Greetings from Asbury Park, N.J.*, just as the city fell on hard times. The Stone Pony bar where Springsteen performed during this period is still there as a club. Since 2005 the city's beachfront has undergone revitalization with new restaurants, vibrant small business, and refurbished buildings.

1901

COLEMAN HOUSE, ASBURY PARK
Oscar Wilde once stayed at the Coleman House Hotel

ABOVE: The Coleman House, in 1901, was at one time Asbury Park's largest and best-known hotel taking up an entire block on the corner of Asbury Avenue and Ocean Avenue, just set back from the beach. The hotel was built by John Cook for Sarah Coleman, opening in July 1879. It was enlarged in 1880 and 1888. The hotel was regularly featured in the *New York Times* as the newspaper reported on important guests arriving and the hotel's various social activities. Irish playwright Oscar Wilde stayed here in 1888 while on a lecture tour, as did well-known yachtsman and challenger for the America's Cup Sir Thomas Lipton. Many hotels offered social functions aimed at much younger guests. The Coleman House, for example, was the site one year of the Queen's Coronation Ball, a highlight of the Asbury Park's children's carnival. The early 1900s was a period when Asbury Park was a popular destination, served by the Central Railroad of New Jersey and the Pennsylvania Railroad.

ABOVE: During the first decade of the twentieth century a number of notables stayed at Coleman House, including U.S. Presidents Ulysses Grant, Woodrow Wilson, and Herbert Hoover. Sarah Coleman sold her hotel in 1911. In 1917, when A. M. Sexton was proprietor, Coleman House advertised itself as a magnificent hotel with an unobstructed view of Boardwalk and Ocean; commending itself to people "of refinement." Today, the Empress Hotel occupies the site of the former Coleman House Hotel which was torn down in 1934 after a number of years of declining revenue. The site was a parking lot until construction of the Empress Hotel in 1959. The Empress Hotel has 101 guest rooms and still offers views of the boardwalk and beach. It was extensively refurbished in 2004. The hotel's nightclub was a shore pioneer when it began offering gay entertainment in 1997, although the hotel itself has diverse clientele.

1934

SS *MORRO CASTLE*, BEACHED AT ASBURY PARK
The devastating fire aboard *Morro Castle* was a catalyst for improved shipboard fire safety

ABOVE: The SS *Morro Castle* was a Ward Line cruise ship which regularly sailed from New York City to Havana, Cuba. She was launched in March 1930 at 508 feet long and 11,520 gross tons (in comparison, the RMS *Titanic* was 882 feet long). A fire was discovered as the ship passed Long Beach Island, New Jersey, with the ship finally running aground in Asbury Park near the convention

center after blazing for many hours. The rescuers were slow to react. The first rescue ship to arrive on the scene was the SS *Andrea F. Luckenbach*. Two other ships—the SS *Monarch* of Bermuda and the SS *City of Savannah*—were slow in taking action after receiving the S.O.S. signal. A fourth ship to participate in the rescue operations was the SS *President Cleveland*. The Coast Guard vessels

Tampa and *Cahoone* positioned themselves too far away to see the victims in the water and rendered little assistance. The Coast Guard's aerial station at Cape May, New Jersey, failed to send their float planes until local radio stations started reporting dead bodies were washing ashore on the New Jersey beaches. In all, 135 passengers and crew perished out of 549 onboard.

ABOVE: Harry Moore, governor of New Jersey, helped boats locate survivors and bodies by dipping the wings of his plane and dropping markers.

BELOW: *Morro Castle* burned at sea for three days. Only six of the ship's twelve lifeboats were launched and although the combined capacity of these boats was 408, they carried only eighty-five people.

ABOVE: After a hearing on the *Morro Castle* disaster, the Steamboat Inspection Service concluded there was no formal effort to fight the fire, crew failed to aid passengers, and no effort was made to use backup emergency steering or lighting power. The disaster led to several safety-at-sea initiatives, including restricting use of flammable material in cabins and public areas, installing automatic fire doors and ship-wide fire alarms. The fire's cause has never been truly determined. The ship was grounded on the Asbury Park beach, just offshore from the Convention Hall, and was a tourist attraction for three months or so after the fire, until the hulk was towed to the scrap yard. The Convention Hall—shown in many news photos of the beached ship—was designed by Whitney, Warren, and Charles Wetmore, the same architects who designed New York's Grand Central Station. The steel-frame building with brick walls and terra-cotta decorations was completed in 1930, and was designed to have the boardwalk run though its central arcade. It has recently been refurbished.

1938

SHARK RIVER DRAWBRIDGE
One of New Jersey's busiest drawbridges

ABOVE: The drawbridge pictured in this 1938 photo is on Ocean Avenue and spans the Shark River, which divides Belmar from Avon-by-the-Sea. The two-lane drawbridge, with pedestrian walkways and two symmetrical control towers, is technically known as a double-leaf bascule bridge. It is made of steel and consists of three spans for a total length of 339 feet, with a width of forty feet. The two-story concrete operator's houses on opposite sides of the drawbridge are art deco in style.

ABOVE: The bridge on Ocean Avenue is one the state's busiest drawbridges. Engineers call these bridges "movable spans" because there are other types of movable bridges other than drawbridges. Shark River drawbridge opens more than 8,000 times a year according to the state Department of Transportation (DOT). The bridge also attracts its share of summertime spectators who watch as the bridge gracefully rises to let a fishing boat or sailboat come from the Atlantic Ocean into Shark River, which leads into Belmar Harbor. The bridge was extensively rebuilt in 1987 with new decking, many movable parts replaced, electrical systems upgraded, and automated traffic signals and control gates added.

1935

THE *HINDENBURG* AT LAKEHURST
The disaster that marked the end of passenger-carrying airships

ABOVE: The fiery crash of the German grand zeppelin *Hindenburg* on its landing at Lakehurst Naval Air Station on Thursday, May 6, 1937, put an end to the airship era. Hydrogen gas explosion and subsequent rapidly spreading fire engulfed the dirigible as it attempted to tie up to the mooring mast, killing thirteen passengers, twenty-two air crew, and one ground crew. The airship normally carried seventy passengers, but only had thirty-six passengers on this trip. The zeppelin had already made a successful round trip to Brazil that season but had been delayed on its flight from Frankfurt and had flown over

Manhattan on its route to Lakehurst. When it arrived, there were additional delays while it circled off the New Jersey coast allowing a local storm at the naval base to pass. Radio announcer Herb Morrison of Chicago station WSL was at Lakehurst describing the landing and described the season vividly: "It's burning and bursting into flames … it's falling on the mooring mast … this is the one of the worst catastrophes in the world. It's a terrific crash, ladies and gentlemen. It's smoke, and it's in flames now; and the frame is crashing to the ground, not quite to the mooring mast. Oh, the humanity!"

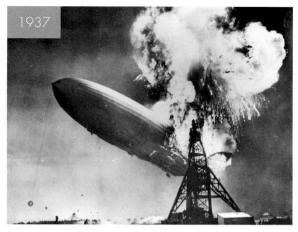

1937

ABOVE: The *Hindenburg* tragedy wasn't the first airship disaster to strike New Jersey. Four years earlier the USS *Akron* was lost after ditching into the sea off the Jersey coast with seventy-three of the seventy-six crew killed, mostly through drowning and hypothermia.

1936

ABOVE: Lakehurst today is still a naval facility under Naval Air Systems Command. Hangar One, which housed the *Hindenburg* when it was here, once again hosts a dirigible. The Navy's first blimp in more than fifty years went into service in 2011 as a research vessel. It is 180 feet long compared to *Hindenburg's* 804-foot length. Hangar One was built in 1920 and is a mammoth 961 feet long, 350 feet wide, and 200 feet tall. It was made a National Historic Landmark in 1968. Lakehurst was the only landing field in the United States

LEFT AND FAR LEFT: The *Hindenburg* on its inaugural visit to Lakehurst in 1936.

RIGHT: Today the crash site has a memorial plaque to the victims and one groundcrew who were killed, with ceremonies taking place to mark the fiftieth and seventy-fifth anniversary. Ironically, more were killed in the USS *Akron* than the *Hindenburg*.

that could be used by commercial dirigibles. Theories abound but the exact cause of the *Hindenburg* crash has never been fully determined. German and American investigations in the crash's aftermath detected no signs of sabotage. Film and audio of the *Hindenburg* crash have been widely seen because newspaper, newsreel, and radio reporters were at Lakehurst for the inaugural U.S. flight of the 1937 season.

c.1920

BARNEGAT LIGHTHOUSE
Unofficial symbol of the state of New Jersey

ABOVE: Barnegat Lighthouse was an important lighthouse at the northern tip of Long Beach Island. Some mariners argued in the early twentieth century that Barnegat Light and Fire Island Lighthouse on Long Island were the true marker beacons for New York Harbor as mariners lined up on them far out to sea navigating their entry into the harbor. At the lighthouse's base is an unusual triple keepers' dwelling built in 1889. Barnegat had three keepers, a larger than usual staff as most lighthouses only had a keeper and assistant. The current lighthouse was built in 1859 replacing an 1834 lighthouse that was inadequate and later swept into the sea. The lighthouse was designed by George Gordon Meade who would become a successful Union Army general and a significant figure at Gettysburg a few years later. Meade also designed Absecon Lighthouse in Atlantic City. Both are tall, narrow towers rising from flat sandy beaches. Barnegat Light is 161 feet tall and displayed a first order Fresnel lens.

RIGHT: Barnegat Lighthouse, the state's unofficial symbol, is depicted on license plates and is popularly known as Old Barney. The lighthouse overlooks the rough waters of the Inlet at the northern end of Long Beach Island. In seventeenth-century Dutch, Barnegat means "breakers inlet." The lighthouse has been in constant conflict with the sea as rock jetties have been built over the years to protect the lighthouse. The lighthouse was taken over by the state in 1926 after it was replaced by a lightship, which in turn was replaced by a large anchored buoy in 1969. It has been a state park since 1974.

1898

SANDY HOOK LIGHTHOUSE
New Jersey's pre-Revolutionary lighthouse

LEFT: Sandy Hook Lighthouse, the nation's oldest lighthouse, is still an active aid to navigation overlooking the Sandy Hook Peninsula and outer New York Harbor. It has been shining a light since June 11, 1764. The keepers' house was built in 1883. The lighthouse is made of brick and was built by Isaac Conroe. It stands 103 feet tall and has a third order Fresnel lens. An 1852 lighthouse service report sums up its value for much of its existence: "Sandy Hook's main light and the two beacons adjacent serve as the principal guide to pilots and navigators leading from the sea into New York Bay (outer New York Harbor)." The two beacons the report refers to were built in 1817 and served as range lights guiding ships into Sandy Hook Channel leading into New York Harbor. A range is two or more lights in a straight line with the rear light always higher than the front light. Navigators line the rear light over the front range to know they are in the proper position.

ABOVE: The Sandy Hook Peninsula is part of Gateway National Recreation Area, with the beaches, hiking trails, Fort Hancock, and the lighthouse as major attractions. The national park was created in 1972. The lighthouse is on the grounds of former Fort Hancock, a coastal defense fort that guarded New York Harbor from the 1870s to 1974; the Army's Proving Ground was also located at the fort from 1874 to 1919 when it moved to Aberdeen, Maryland. Two smaller lighthouses—or beacons—that operated in conjunction with the Sandy Hook Lighthouse as range lights were decommissioned years ago. One of them became famous as the lighthouse in the popular children's book, *The Little Red House And the Great Grey Bridge*, written in 1942. The lighthouse stands directly below the George Washington Bridge—the Great Grey Bridge—where it was moved to from Sandy Hook. When the United States government was formed in 1789 there were twelve colonial lighthouses, only Sandy Hook remains. New Jersey had thirty-eight lighthouses at one time; eighteen are still standing.

RENAULT WINERY
"Champagne" comes to New Jersey

LEFT: The twenty-four-feet-high concrete champagne bottle on Route 9 in New Gretna, was one of eighty promotional champagne bottles placed adjacent to busy roadways in New Jersey, Florida, California, and Massachusetts. They were part of a 1920s advertising campaign by Renault Winery promoting their champagne. Louis Renault, an immigrant from the Marne, in the Champagne region of France, founded the vineyard in 1864. The Egg Harbor City winery— the state's oldest— produced its first vintages under Monsieur Renault in 1870. Renault won a prize for his wine at the Philadelphia Centennial in 1876. The winery (and the brand) was sold to the D'Agostino family in 1919. The vineyard survived prohibition under the helm of John D'Agostino by selling sacramental wines and also Renault Wine Tonic, licensed by the government. The tonic was sold in drugstores nationwide and had a 22 percent alcoholic content. After prohibition ended, the company bought two California wineries blending their wine with local Labrusca wine, creating a distinctive champagnelike sparkling wine that was sold nationally.

1909

RIGHT: From the 1940s to the 1960s Renault was a major champagne producer, even advertising on the popular Johnny Carson Show. In the 1960s, the state was the ninth largest wine producer, with more than 900,000 gallons sold. Competition from California ate into Renault champagne sales and a change in owners created a new winery focus. The winery has been owned by Joseph Milza since 1977 and the emphasis now is on the winery's eighteen-hole golf course and its hotel, the fifty-room Tuscan House (pictured below). There are forty-two acres of vineyards and the gourmet restaurant and winery tours are still popular. Today wine is making a comeback in the state and is the fastest-growing agricultural segment with thirty-nine wineries. Another fourteen winery applications are pending. In 2010, the latest available data, the state produced 341,000 gallons of wine. The days when a wine critic called New Jersey wines Parkway reds and Turnpike whites is gone forever as many wineries produce excellent wines. New Jersey ranks seventh nationally as a wine producer.

LEFT, BELOW: A rare photo of founder Louis Renault at work in the vaulted room used for aging wine.

BELOW: The winery's Tuscon House hotel.

1938

ATLANTIC CITY BOARDWALK

Originally built to help hotel owners keep sand out of their lobbies, it soon became a major tourist attraction

ABOVE: Atlantic City's famed boardwalk, in 1938, had a Miss America sign displayed because final judging for the beauty pageant was about to begin. The boardwalk was first opened to the public in June 26, 1870. It was the idea of a railroad conductor—Alexander Boardman—who was tired of sweeping sand from his passenger cars. Train service to Atlantic City had begun in 1854. Several hotels supported the boardwalk idea because they too were tired of sweeping sand out of their lobbies. The first boardwalk was a simple arrangement of planks laid on the beach that were four feet wide and taken up at the end of the season. That simple development led, by the 1930s, to a boardwalk that was sixty feet wide made of steel and concrete construction, overlaid with pine planking in a herringbone pattern. From the earliest days, amusement piers jutted out from the Boardwalk into the Atlantic Ocean. Steel Pier, Million Dollar Pier, Heinz Pier, Garden Pier, and others, offered concerts, amusements, and attractions such as Steel Pier's famous diving horse.

c.1905

c.1905

LEFT AND TOP LEFT: The boardwalk afforded visitors the chance to promenade close to the sea or have the luxury of being pushed in a rolling chair.

ABOVE: "Atlantic City is an amusement factory operated on a straight line mass production pattern. The belt is the boardwalk," is how the WPA Guide to New Jersey described the boardwalk in the late 1930s. That description would be true into the late 1950s. Today the boardwalk is a shadow of its former glory, although it still attracts thousands on a summer day. The boardwalk is about 5.1 miles long to the Ventnor town line; in the 1930s it was more than seven miles long. Atlantic City thrived in an era when people took trains to resorts before jet airplane travel and before widespread ownership of cars and the advent of express highways. The boardwalk is also impacted by declining visits to casinos as other states have permitted casino gambling, cutting into Atlantic City's crowds. The famous Miss America pageant left Atlantic City in 2004, after being held at the Convention Center on the boardwalk since 1921. Some innovations survive: the Boardwalk's rolling chairs, Jitney Bus service, and saltwater taffy remain.

c.1900

RESORTS CASINO
Continuing Atlantic City's luxury hotel and entertainment tradision

ABOVE: The Haddon Hall Hotel on North Carolina Avenue in Atlantic City was founded in 1869 by Samuel and Susanna Hunt. They named it after the Quaker family who had founded Haddonfield, New Jersey. In 1890, the Leeds & Lippincott Company bought the hotel. They substantially renovated and enlarged the hotel and also moved it closer to the Boardwalk,

reopening in March 1896. The now four-story Haddon Hall could accommodate 400 guests. In 1900 Leeds & Lippincott bought the neighboring Chalfonte House. They built Atlantic City's first skyscraper on its site, the ten-story Chalfonte Hotel, which opened July 2, 1904. To compete with its across-the-street neighbor, Haddon Hall began a major expansion program in the 1920s,

with two eleven-story additions and a center tower, completed in 1929. That same year Haddon Hall and Chalfonte Hotel merged creating Atlantic City's largest hotel with 1,000 rooms. The two hotels were connected by an overhead walkway. The combined facilities became known as the Chalfonte-Haddon Hall Hotel.

1915

1915

ABOVE: The ten-story Chalfonte Hotel. Haddon Hall is on the right in the top photo.

ABOVE: During World War II many Atlantic City hotels were taken over by the military and became known as Camp Boardwalk. Chalfonte-Haddon Hall Hotel was renamed for the war as Thomas England General Hospital. From June 1942 until November 1946, the hospital treated more than 4,500 war casualties. Today's Resorts Hotel & Casino is an amalgam of additions and modifications of the original Haddon Hall Hotel. Resorts was Atlantic City's first casino, opening on May 26, 1978. Resorts cut the number of rooms to about 550 from the earlier 1,000 rooms. The Chalfonte Hotel was torn down in 1980; it had been vacant and the site was turned into a parking lot. Haddon Hall was the basis of the Resorts Hotel & Casino because it was a newer construction, it was easier to convert to modern use, and it had space for a large casino on the ground floor as well as room for shops and restaurants. It has had several owners, including television personality the late Merv Griffin, since its opening and is now owned by the Gomes family.

1900

VIEW FROM ABSECON LIGHTHOUSE
Atlantic City's lighthouse has been aiding navigators for over 150 years

ABOVE: The vista from the lantern room on top of Absecon Lighthouse on Vermont Avenue in Atlantic City in 1900 looked basically the same for more than a century. Garden Pier was always in view, with midrise apartment buildings and hotels, and smaller two- to three-story buildings. The lighthouse was a popular tourist attraction at the turn of the twentieth century receiving more than 10,000 visitors annually, with keepers often complaining that tending to visitors kept them from their duties. The lighthouse was put into service on January 15, 1857, and was 171 feet tall with a first-order Fresnel lens. It cost $52,187 to build. Absecon, tall and slender, looks like Cape

May and Barnegat Lighthouse. They were all built at roughly the same time and two of the designers and builders—George Gordon Meade and Lieutenant Colonel William F. Reynolds—had a hand in all three. The driving force behind the lighthouse was Dr. Jonathan Pitney, founder of Atlantic City in the 1850s.

1900

RIGHT: Absecon Lighthouse around 1900. The similarity with Barnegat Lighthouse is not accidental.

RIGHT: The newly completed Revel Hotel and Casino imposes itself on the view from the lighthouse. Revel is Atlantic City's twelfth casino. Casino gambling came to Atlantic City following a statewide referendum in 1976. The first casino opened on May 26, 1978, when Resorts Hotel and Casino began business. Governor Brendan Byrne cut the opening blue ribbon. Gambling was supposed to revitalize Atlantic City, which had fallen on hard times as vacationers went to Florida and other sunny climes with more modern hotels. The city's population was 27,838 in 1900; in its heyday in 1930 there were 66,198 people, dropping to 40,199 in 1970; today it is 39,558. The city is again facing problems as millions of its former visitors gamble at casinos closer to home. The boardwalk is still an attraction and the lighthouse, which had a million dollar plus facelift and the construction of a replica keepers cottage in the late 1990s, draws lighthouse fans.

c.1970

LUCY THE ELEPHANT, MARGATE
The residents of Margate never forget their elephant

ABOVE: Lucy the Elephant has graced the Margate oceanfront on Atlantic Avenue since 1882 when Philadelphia real estate speculator James V. Lafferty put her there to aid in land sales. Lucy was designed by Philadelphia architect William Free and cost $25,000 to build. She was one of three elephants Lafferty built—one in Coney Island, the other in Lower Township, neither survived. Lafferty received a U.S. government patent for Lucy on December 5, 1882. The elephant served as an office, an attention getter, and also a viewing platform where potential buyers could see their building lots. Anton Gertzen of Philadelphia bought Lucy in 1887, and in subsequent years she became everything from a tavern to a hotel to a private home. Lucy is built of sheet metal over a wooden frame and is 65 feet high from her toenails to the top of the howdah, the decorative seat on her back. She weighs about ninety tons. The legs contain stairs leading onto the body.

ABOVE: The ponderous pachyderm was moved two blocks south on Atlantic Avenue to its present location on July 20, 1970, following its rescue by the Save Lucy Committee. The Gertzen family, who owned Lucy, sold their land to developers and donated Lucy to the city of Margate. Lucy had to be moved or she would be torn down; this threat led to the formation of the Save Lucy Committee. Lucy needed immediate repairs to her structure and also cosmetic work, and after the first phase of rehabilitation, she reopened in 1974. Lucy's further refurbishment took place in stages, and by 1976 the sheet metal skin had been replaced and a new howdah was installed. In the early 1980s the interior was refurbished. Lucy's renovations over the years cost about $600,000. On May 11, 1976, Lucy was designated a National Historic Landmark. The award cited: "(Lucy) is the last survivor of what historians call 'zoomorphic architecture.' Built as an architectural folly to attract home buyers to the area." She is now a museum and popular tourist attraction.

c.1940

VICTORIAN ARCHITECTURE, CAPE MAY

A major factor in granting Cape May its National Historic Landmark status

ABOVE: Cape May's Victorian architecture—shown here on Congress Place—consists of many styles ranging from Second Empire, Queen Anne, Richardson Romanesque, Gothic Revival to Italianate. Cape May was one of the country's first resorts. It became a popular escape from city crowds and noise after excursion boat service was inaugurated from Philadelphia down the Delaware River in the 1830s. The country's largest hotel, the Mount Vernon Hotel, was here until an 1856 fire destroyed it. Fire was a constant threat; a major fire in 1878 almost destroyed the town tourist economy. It raged for eleven hours on November 8, 1878, first taking hold at 7 a.m. in the attic of the new wing at Ocean House on Perry Street. By the time the flames could be contained, some forty acres of prime property lay in a pile of charred ruins.

c.1930

ABOVE: When Cape May City was granted National Historic Landmark status on May 11, 1976, the award said in part, "With over 600 summer homes, hotels and commercial structures, this venerable seashore resort has one of the largest collections of nineteenth-century frame buildings remaining in the United States." The buildings erected after the fire—at the height of Victorian architecture in the United States—provided the basis for the town's resurgence a century later. The buildings were preserved because Cape May became surpassed by other coastal resorts, notably Atlantic City, and was a backwater fishing port off the main tourist routes. Many of the old Victorian homes became bed and breakfasts. A renewed interest in quaint and distinctive places spurred on tourism. Recently the National Park Service put Cape May's Landmark status on its watch list, meaning "the landmark faces impending actions or circumstances that will likely cause a loss of integrity." Critics have complained of inappropriate development.

LEFT: The view from 901–931 Beach Avenue.

SEASIDE HEIGHTS AFTER THE SUPERSTORM

Taking the brunt of Superstorm Sandy

2012

LEFT: Summer fun at Seaside Heights with Casino Pier and its famous Jet Star roller coaster in the background. The mid-New Jersey shore community has billed itself as a family resort since its founding in 1913, but it also attracts large numbers of young people with its bars and clubs as well as a two-mile boardwalk, originally built between 1916 and 1921, that focuses on amusements, rides, and food vendors. Two of the boardwalk's major attractions are piers extending into the ocean, Casino Pier and Funtown Pier. Casino Pier was founded in 1932 by Linus Gilbert, a Princeton contractor who purchased and restored a fire-damaged Dentzel carousel from Burlington Island Park, making it the main attraction for the developing amusement area at the north end of the boardwalk. Gilbert's carousel was originally housed in an open-sided building, but weather damage and complaints about the organ noise inspired Gilbert to purchase the pier and expand the attractions, enclosing the carousel in a larger arcade complex. After that, the pier went through several owners until it was acquired in 2002 by the Storino family, owners of Jenkinson's Boardwalk in nearby Point Pleasant Beach. Seaside Heights has a year-round population of 2,887 swelling to 65,000 on summer weekends. It has gained national publicity as the site of the popular reality television show, *Jersey Shore*.

BOTTOM LEFT AND RIGHT: Superstorm Sandy swept into Seaside Heights, ripping up the boardwalk and causing extensive damage to its two amusement piers. In the aerial photograph (right), heavily damaged Funtown Pier with its Ferris wheel appears at the bottom of the photo, while Casino Pier is shown at the top. The Jet Star roller coaster, along with the end of the 300-foot Casino Pier, was plunged into the Atlantic Ocean with the roller coaster landing upright, its stark framework creating an iconic storm-damage picture. The boardwalk has been almost destroyed twice in the past—first by The Great Atlantic Hurricane of 1944, then by a catastrophic fire in 1955. Seaside Heights Mayor Bill Akers predicts it will cost $13 million to replace the boardwalk. Completion of construction is expected by May 2013, in time for the summer tourist season, which generates 75 percent of the town's revenue. Overall damage in the borough was estimated at $1 billion. Damage to Casino Pier was estimated at $45 million, which includes removing the roller coaster from the ocean. While Casino Pier will likely be replaced, Funtown Pier's owners are still deciding what the future holds. Either way, the tradition of going "down the shore" in the summertime will surely continue.

SPRING LAKE AFTER SUPERSTORM SANDY

Miles of boardwalk disappeared overnight along the New Jersey shoreline

BELOW: The northern shore community of Spring Lake in the 1920s with the new Monmouth Hotel—then one of the town's most prestigious establishments—directly behind the boardwalk. Philadelphians created the resort in 1875 and officially incorporated it in 1892 at the height of the Gilded Age with homes designed by leading Philadelphia architects. Spring Lake is about sixty-five miles south of New York City and the same distance east of Philadelphia. To enhance the town's natural beauty, a two-mile long boardwalk was built facing the Atlantic Ocean. Besides its historic boardwalk, the upscale community, with 3,000 year-round residents, has two buildings on the National Register of Historic Places: Normandy Inn and Holy Trinity Episcopal Church. Spring Lake was the site of several notorious shark attacks during the summer of 1916 that are said to have inspired the Peter Benchley novel *Jaws*.

RIGHT: Mantoloking, one of the communities on narrow, sandy Barnegat Peninsula, about seven miles north of Seaside Heights, was hard-hit with many homes destroyed as shown in the aerial photograph; County Route 528 bridge is in the center. A wealthy community of only 300 residents, Mantoloking was known for its shingle-style houses overlooking the ocean and bay. Damage along the coast was not consistent with some towns suffering little or no damage. Experts said the extent of damage depended mostly on beach and dune contours, i.e., wide beaches and high dunes offered protection, and on the wind speed and direction as well as ocean floor contours.

c.1925

LEFT: Only concrete supports remain for Spring Lake's two miles of boardwalk that was ripped from its base and swept out to sea, or in some cases hurled blocks inland, as Sandy came ashore on October 29, 2012. The town plans to rebuild the boardwalk. Farther south, towns on slender Barnegat Peninsula, such as Bay Head, Mantoloking, Ortley Beach, and Seaside Heights, suffered extensive damage as the Atlantic Ocean swept over the peninsula into Barnegat Bay destroying hundred of homes and damaging many more. It wasn't only shore towns that suffered; communities along the Hudson and Hackensack rivers flooded as part of the tidal surge. Approximately 2.7 million people lost power in New Jersey, with many homes affected for two weeks or more. There were thirty storm-related deaths and property damage was placed at $39.6 billion. The governor's office estimated that 350,000 homes in the state suffered significant damage—ten percent of the state's housing.